Tribology in Sustainable Composites

Tribological performance of sustainable composites depend upon external parameters such as interface and environmental temperature, contact pressure and behavior of contact materials at interface and so forth. This book covers sustainable composites and bio-composites in terms of proper selection of reinforcements, methods to improve the thermal and mechanical properties, techniques for uniform dispersion of the reinforcements and their tribological performance. Also, it details the testing and damage characterization methods of these sustainable composites.

Features:

1. Presents fundamental knowledge of sustainable composites, including chemical composition, structural features and fabrication techniques.
2. Provides an analytical overview of the different types of characterization techniques and tribological methods.
3. Provides an extensive review on bio-composite properties and their tribological performance for biomedical application.
4. Contains extensive reviews on cutting-edge research on lightweight materials for future applications in a variety of industries and their tribological performance.
5. Provides the application of sustainable composites in various fields such as aerospace, automobile, medical etc.

This book is aimed for Researchers, Professionals and Graduate students of Tribology, Composites, Mechanical Engineering and Materials Engineering.

Tribology in Sustainable Composites

Jitendra Kumar Katiyar
Mohammed Abdul Samad

CRC Press is an imprint of the
Taylor & Francis Group, an **informa** business

Cover image: metamorworks/Shutterstock

First edition published 2023
by CRC Press
6000 Broken Sound Parkway NW, Suite 300, Boca Raton, FL 33487-2742

and by CRC Press
4 Park Square, Milton Park, Abingdon, Oxon, OX14 4RN

CRC Press is an imprint of Taylor & Francis Group, LLC

© 2023 Jitendra Kumar Katiyar and Mohammed Abdul Samad

Reasonable efforts have been made to publish reliable data and information, but the author and publisher cannot assume responsibility for the validity of all materials or the consequences of their use. The authors and publishers have attempted to trace the copyright holders of all material reproduced in this publication and apologize to copyright holders if permission to publish in this form has not been obtained. If any copyright material has not been acknowledged please write and let us know so we may rectify in any future reprint.

Except as permitted under U.S. Copyright Law, no part of this book may be reprinted, reproduced, transmitted, or utilized in any form by any electronic, mechanical, or other means, now known or hereafter invented, including photocopying, microfilming, and recording, or in any information storage or retrieval system, without written permission from the publishers.

For permission to photocopy or use material electronically from this work, access www.copyright.com or contact the Copyright Clearance Center, Inc. (CCC), 222 Rosewood Drive, Danvers, MA 01923, 978-750-8400. For works that are not available on CCC please contact mpkbookspermissions@tandf.co.uk

Trademark notice: Product or corporate names may be trademarks or registered trademarks and are used only for identification and explanation without intent to infringe.

ISBN: 978-1-032-22040-6 (hbk)
ISBN: 978-1-032-22041-3 (pbk)
ISBN: 978-1-003-27096-6 (ebk)

DOI: 10.1201/9781003270966

Typeset in Times
by Newgen Publishing UK

Contents

Preface...ix
About the Authors..xi

Chapter 1 Sustainable Composites...1

    1.1   Background...1
    1.2   Introduction...1
            1.2.1   Kenaf (*Hibiscus cannabinus*)...............................3
            1.2.2   Hemp (*Cannabis sativa*).....................................3
            1.2.3   Jute (*Corchorus capsularis*)................................3
            1.2.4   Flax (*Linum usitatissimum*).................................5
            1.2.5   Ramie (*Boehmeria nivea*)....................................5
            1.2.6   Nettle (*Urtica dioica*)...5
            1.2.7   Pineapple Leaf (*Ananas comosus*).......................5
            1.2.8   Sisal (*Agave sisalana*)...6
            1.2.9   Date Palm (*Phoenix dactylifera*)..........................6
            1.2.10 Coconut Fiber (*Cocos nucifera*)..........................6
            1.2.11 Kapok (*Ceiba pentandra*)....................................6
            1.2.12 Bamboo (*Bambusoideae*)....................................6
            1.2.13 Silk (*Bombyx mori*)..7
            1.2.14 Cotton (*Gossipiyum*)..7
    1.3   Properties of Natural Fibers...7
    1.4   Advantages of Natural Fiber Composites..........................7
    1.5   Disadvantages of Natural Fiber Composites....................11
    1.6   Extraction of Natural Fibers...11
    1.7   Fabrication Techniques...11
    1.8   Characterization of Natural Fiber Composites.................11
            1.8.1   Morphological Observation...................................16
            1.8.2   Physical Properties..16
            1.8.3   Thermal Behavior..17
            1.8.4   Mechanical Performance.......................................18
                    1.8.4.1   Tensile Test......................................18
                    1.8.4.2   Flexural Test.....................................19
                    1.8.4.3   Impact Test.......................................19
                    1.8.4.4   Compressive Strength........................19
                    1.8.4.5   Hardness Test....................................19
                    1.8.4.6   Crashworthiness................................19
             1.8.5   Tribological Performance......................................20

v

1.9	Possibilities to Improve the Properties of Natural Fibers		24
	1.9.1	Physical Treatment	24
	1.9.2	Chemical Treatment	25
		1.9.2.1 Alkaline Treatment	25
		1.9.2.2 Silane Treatment	25
		1.9.2.3 Acetylation Treatment	26
		1.9.2.4 Peroxide Treatment	26
		1.9.2.5 Benzoylation Treatment	26
		1.9.2.6 Potassium Permanganate ($KMnO_4$) Treatment	26
		1.9.2.7 Stearic Acid Treatment	26
		1.9.2.8 Functionalization of Polymers and Natural Fibers	31
1.10	Factors Affecting the Performance of Natural Fibers Reinforced Composites (NFRCs)		33
1.11	Applications of Natural Fibers		35
1.12	Sustainability of Natural Fiber Reinforced Composites (NFRCs)		35
	1.12.1 Environmental Perspective		36
	1.12.2 Economic Perspective		37
1.13	Biodegradability of Sustainable Composites		38
1.14	Future Trends and Challenges		38
1.15	Summary		39

Chapter 2 Factors Affecting the Properties of Sustainable Composites 45

2.1	Introduction	45
2.2	Fiber Concentration	45
2.3	Fiber Orientation	48
2.4	Fiber Dispersion	51
2.5	Fiber Treatment	51
2.6	Effect of Nano Material in Natural Fiber Composite	52
2.7	Life-Cycle Assessment of Natural Fiber Reinforced Composites (NFRCs)	52
2.8	Summary	52

Chapter 3 Tribological Behavior of Sustainable Composites 61

3.1	Introduction		61
3.2	Sustainable Metallic Composites		62
	3.2.1	Fabrication Techniques of Metallic Sustainable Composites	62
	3.2.2	Tribological Characterization of Metallic Sustainable Composites	67

Contents   vii

        3.2.3   Wear Mechanisms Observed in Metallic Sustainable Composites 67

3.3   Sustainable Polymer Composites 68

        3.3.1   Effect of Fiber Orientations on Tribological Properties 68

        3.3.2   Effect of Fiber Orientations and Treatment on the Tribological Properties 72

        3.3.3   Effect of Operating Conditions on the Tribological Properties 73

        3.3.4   Wear Mechanisms Observed in Polymer Sustainable Composites 73

3.4   Comparison of the Tribological Properties of a Few Polymer Sustainable Composites 75

3.5   Conclusion and Future Prospects 76

Chapter 4   Applications of Sustainable Composites 79

4.1   Introduction 79

4.2   Applications of Sustainable Composites 82

        4.2.1   Sustainable Composites in Civil Structures 82

        4.2.2   Sustainable Composites in Automobile Industry 82

        4.2.3   Sustainable Composites in Medical Industry 83

        4.2.4   Sustainable Composites for Energy Applications 85

        4.2.5   Sustainable Composites for Miscellaneous Applications 88

4.3   Summary 89

Index 93

Preface

One of the biggest challenges engineers face during the design process is the proper selection of materials as some components may demand materials with conflicting properties, such as light weight with significant strength or brittleness with excellent toughness/stiffness/fatigue resistance. In order to overcome these challenges, researchers have developed composites in the recent past, which give engineers the option to choose materials with the desired competitive properties. Composites are defined as a mixture of two or more distinct materials, which are bonded chemically at a microscopic scale. One of the constituents of the composite material, which is continuous and available in large quantity, is called the matrix, and the other constituent, which is added to the matrix, is called reinforcement or filler. A metal, ceramic or a polymer may be used as a matrix. If a metal is used, it is called metal matrix composite (MMC). Likewise, if a polymer or ceramic is used as a matrix, it is known as a polymer matrix composite (PMC) or ceramic matrix composite (CMC), respectively. Furthermore, based upon their shape and size, reinforcements or the fillers are classified into several categories, such as particulate, whisker and short/long fiber.

Among all types of composite materials, carbon and glass fiber reinforced composite materials have been used for many years in several different types of applications. However, these conventional composites are derived from non-renewable reinforcements and they pose a significant threat to the environment. Government legislation and consumer behavior have recently forced many industries to adapt sustainable composites. Industries such as automotive, marine and aerospace are now seeking sustainable lightweight composites with the aim to reduce the overall weight of the components with enhanced materials and design aspects. Therefore, there is high demand on research for the development of sustainable composites. Notwithstanding the development attained, there are substantial obstacles to the simplification of structural applications of composite materials. This is mainly due to their high cost and complex mechanical behavior. In fact, there is presently deficient knowledge related to mechanical properties and failure/wear mechanisms of composites prepared from renewable sources.

Furthermore, due to the ever-increasing need for reducing the weight of components, the demand for developing lightweight composites without compromising on the mechanical and thermal properties is continuously growing. Moreover, the use of bio-composites in industries such as medical, automotive and aerospace is on the rise because of environmental and health issues. However, there are numerous challenges to overcome before these composites find their place in real applications. Among all challenges, tribological performance is the biggest one. Tribological study covers friction, wear and lubrication with the necessary involvement of different researchers. It is more important to note that the tribological performance of sustainable composites largely depends upon external parameters. Only a few parameters have a greater impact on tribological performance. These are interface and environmental temperature, contact pressure and behavior of contact materials at interface, sliding speed and applied load. Therefore, this book aims to provide comprehensive guide about sustainable composites and bio-composites in terms of proper selection of reinforcements, methods to improve the thermal and mechanical properties of these materials, techniques for uniform dispersion of the reinforcements and their tribological performance. Furthermore, this book aims to provide extensive information about the testing and damage characterization methods for these sustainable composites.

This book could be well suited for undergraduate, post-graduate and professional level courses. The present short form of the book would shed significant light on future trends of sustainable composite materials and their tribological performance, and would be sufficiently readable and thorough in the areas covered. It will aid academicians and scientists who wish to learn more about the nature and prospects of the manufacturing methods, techniques of property enhancement, morphological structures and failure/wear mechanisms for sustainable composite materials.

About the Authors

Jitendra Kumar Katiyar is presently working as a research assistant professor, in the Department of Mechanical Engineering, SRM Institute of Science and Technology, Kattankulathur Chennai, India. His research interests include tribology of carbon materials, polymer composites, self-lubricating polymers, lubrication tribology, modern manufacturing techniques and coatings for advanced technologies. He obtained his bachelor's degree (with honors) from UPTU Lucknow in 2007. He completed his masters and Ph.D. from the Indian Institute of Technology Kanpur, India in 2010 and 2017, respectively. He is the life member of the Tribology Society of India, Malaysian Society of Tribology, Institute of Engineers, India and The Indian Society for Technical Education (ISTE). He has authored/co- authored/published more than 35 articles in reputed journals, 35 articles in international/national conferences, 15 book chapters, 10 books published in CRC Press USA and Springer Nature. Further, he has published a book on Engineering Thermodynamics for UG level with Khanna Publication. He has served as a guest editor for a special issue in journals like *Tribology Materials, Surfaces and Interfaces, Journal of Engineering Tribology Part J, Journal of Process Mechanical Engineering Part E, Arabian Journal for Science and Engineering, Industrial Lubrication and Tribology* and *Frontier in Mechanical Engineering: Tribology*. Further, he is Member Editorial Board in Tribology Materials, Surfaces and Interfaces and Review Editor in Frontier in Mechanical Engineering. He is also an active reviewer in various reputed journals related to materials, manufacturing and tribology. He has delivered more than 35 invited talk on various research fields related to tribology, composite materials, surface engineering and machining. He has organized more than 7 FDP/Short Term Courses and International Tribology Research Symposium in tribology. He has been teaching modern manufacturing technology, computer aided design, computer aided manufacturing, metrology and quality control, basic civil and mechanical engineering, manufacturing technology in UG and tribology in design in PG at SRMIST.

Mohammed Abdul Samad is an associate professor and the Director of Tribology Lab in the ME Department at King Fahd University of Petroleum and Minerals, Dhahran, KSA. He earned his BS in Mechanical Engineering from the University College of Engineering, Osmania University, Hyderabad. He obtained his masters in ME from King Fahd University of Petroleum and Minerals, Saudi Arabia, and joined the department as a lecturer. He earned his Ph.D. in Mechanical Engineering from the National University of Singapore, Singapore. His main research interests include micro\nano tribology, thin films, coatings and nano-composites. He has about 80 journal papers in reputed journals on wide-ranging subjects including polymeric and metal composites. He has handled a guest editorship for a special issue on Tribology in Arabian Journal for Science and Engineering. He is also an active reviewer in various reputed journals. He has delivered several invited talks on various research fields related to tribology, composite materials, surface engineering and machining. He was instrumental in obtaining funding for several research projects from different organizations.

1 Sustainable Composites

1.1 BACKGROUND

In the present time, more attention is being paid to environmental issues. These issues are raised at various levels of academia, industries and environmental organizations. The major concern is the production of non-sustainable products in large volumes and the way they are disposed of. To solve this issue, scientists/researchers are working on alternatives to non-sustainable materials. Also, sustainable materials are becoming more popular each day. This development opens a new field of research which includes many types of sustainable materials that can be used in the mechanical, civil, electrical and medical industries.

1.2 INTRODUCTION

One of the top challenges engineers face during the design process is the proper selection of materials as some components may require materials with conflicting properties, such as light weight with significant strength or brittleness with excellent toughness/stiffness/fatigue resistance. Hence, to overcome these challenges, researchers have been concentrating on the development of composites, which give engineers the ability to select materials competing properties. Composites are defined as a mixture of two or more distinct materials, which are bonded chemically at a microscopic scale. One of the constituents of a composite material, which is continuous and available in large quantities, is referred to as the matrix, while the other, which is added to the matrix, is referred to as the reinforcement or filler. A metal, ceramic or a polymer may be used in the form of a matrix. If a metal is used, it is referred to as a metal matrix composite (MMC). Likewise, if a polymer or ceramic is used as a matrix, then it is known as a polymer matrix composite (PMC) or ceramic matrix composite (CMC), respectively. Furthermore, based upon their shape and size, reinforcements or the fillers are classified into several categories, such as particulate, whisker and short/long fiber. The classification of composites is shown in Figure 1.1.

Carbon and glass fiber reinforced composite materials have been used for many years in different types of applications. But, these conventional composites are derived from non-renewable reinforcements and they pose a significant threat to the environment. As a result, government legislation and consumer behavior

DOI: 10.1201/9781003270966-1

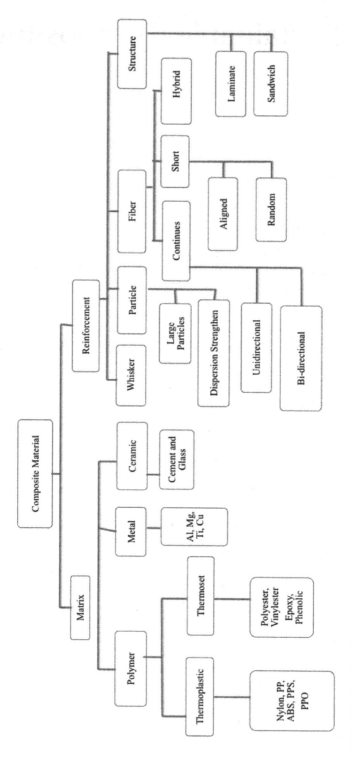

FIGURE 1.1 Classification of composite materials. (Katiyar et al. 2021)

Sustainable Composites 3

have recently compelled many industries to adopt sustainable composite materials, such as those made from renewable resources. Due to this, automotive, marine and aerospace industries are now looking for sustainable lightweight composites in an effort to reduce component weight with improved materials and designs. Moreover, there is high demand on research for the development of sustainable composites. Despite the advancements, there are still substantial challenges to the simplification of composites for structural applications. This is mainly due to their high cost and complex mechanical behavior of the composites (Lee et al. 2009).

Furthermore, the composite materials, which are reinforced with natural fibers, are known as natural fiber composites or sustainable composites. The natural fibers, which differ by source, consist of plant, animal and mineral fibers. Cotton, ramie, jute, flax, sisal and abaca are some of the natural fibers that fall into the plant fiber category, as shown in Figure 1.2.

Jute, ramie, flax and sisal fibers are widely used in the manufacturing of composites. These are defined in detail in the following sections (Thyavihalli Girijappa et al. 2019).

1.2.1 Kenaf (*Hibiscus cannabinus*)

It holds a critical place in the bast fiber family. It is environmentally friendly and biodegradable. In olden days, it was used for textiles, cords, ropes and storage bags, and Egyptians used it for making boats. It is also known as a fibrous plant that is strong, tough and stiff. Around 4000 years ago, plants of this type were cultivated in Africa, Asia, America and a few parts of Europe. Fibers are extracted from flowers, inner core and outer fiber (called bast) using mechanical fiber separator processes, and the whole stalk is used for pulp. After separation, chemical treatment is performed to separate it from non-fibrous substances such as wax and pectin. Further, treated fibers can be woven into fine fabrics. Currently, they are used in the fabrication of composites with additives/fillers. The developed composites are used in automotive, construction, packaging, furniture, textiles, mats, paper pulp and other industries (Omar et al. 2019; Kipriotis et al. 2015)

1.2.2 Hemp (*Cannabis sativa*)

Hemp plants are found mainly in Asia and Europe. The height and diameter of the plant is 1.2–1.4 m and 2 cm, respectively. The inner layer is enclosed by core and the outer layer by bast fiber, which is attached to the inner layer by pectin (a glue-like substance). A sequence of mechanical processes is used to separate the core and the bast fiber. Afterword, the cleaned core is cut into required sizes and the bast fibers are processed to make yarn or bundles. It is used for manufacturing ropes, textiles, garden mulch and an array of building materials and animal beddings. Further, it can be used to fabricate composites as well (Réquilé et al. 2018).

1.2.3 Jute (*Corchorus capsularis*)

It is found in several parts of Asia including India, China, Myanmar and Bangladesh. It develops up to 15–20 cm in 4 months. The fibers are extracted after 4 months

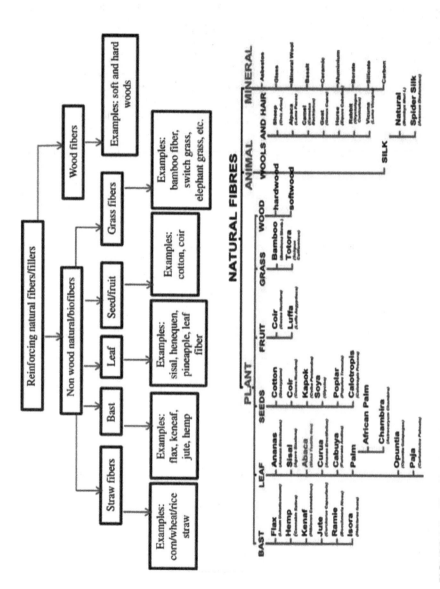

FIGURE 1.2 Classification of natural fibers. (Bhat et al. 2021)

of farming through retting process. The process is carried out either chemically ($N_2H_8C_2O_4$, Na_2SO_3, etc.) or biologically. In biological retting, the stalks are arranged in bundles and kept inside the water for 20 days. This process helps in removing the pectin between core and bast fiber followed by drying of bast fibers. (Shahinur and Hasan 2019).

1.2.4 FLAX (*LINUM USITATISSIMUM*)

The plant comes from the prehistoric period. It looks more crystalline, but it is actually a cellulosic plant. The fibers of the plant (*Linum usitatissimum*) are separated from its stems mainly for producing linen using retting and scorching processes. The length and diameter of the extracted fibers are 90 cm and 12–16 µm, respectively (Ramesh 2019). The plant is found mostly in parts of Europe such as Netherlands, Belgium and France. Further, Canada is the largest flax producer and exporter in the world, producing about 872,000 tons a year (Zafeiropoulos and Baillie 2007). It is used in manufacturing of furniture, textiles, bed sheets, interior decorative accessories, etc.

1.2.5 RAMIE (*BOEHMERIA NIVEA*)

It is a species of herbaceous perennial plants. It is found in China, Japan and Malaysia, and it has been used in textile fabrics for over a century. The plant grows very quickly to a height of 1–2 m and is also known as a non-branching plant. The plant fiber is extracted from the largest and strongest stem and is processed similarly to linen from flex. Fibers can be combined with cotton to fabricate sweaters. Further, it is used in upholstery, gas mantles, fishing nets and marine packing. Moreover, it can be used to fabricate composites that can be used in automotive, furniture, etc. (Bunsell 2018).

1.2.6 NETTLE (*URTICA DIOICA*)

It is a species of herbaceous plants and it is generally available in Europe, Asia, North America and North Africa. It grows up to 2 m in length and have 3–15 cm long leaves, which are soft and green in color. The fiber extraction is carried out during harvesting of flowers using retting process. It is typically used in textile manufacturing, bioenergy, animal housing, etc. (Cummings and Olsen 2011).

1.2.7 PINEAPPLE LEAF (*ANANAS COMOSUS*)

It is an easily available and a richly cultivated plant. Pineapple leaf is a crop waste fiber after cultivation of pineapple. These plants grow up to 1–2 m and have a cluster of leaves (20–30) of about 6 cm in width. It was found that around 90–100 tons of leaves grow per hectare. It is a multicellular and lingo-cellulosic fiber with excellent mechanical properties. It is extracted using a hand scraper. These fibers have a wider application in automobiles, textile, mats, construction, etc. Further, the chemically treated fibers are used for making conveyor belt cords, airbags, advanced composites, etc. (Al-Maharma and Al-Huniti 2019).

6   Tribology in Sustainable Composites

1.2.8 SISAL (*AGAVE SISALANA*)

It is the most commonly used natural fiber and is largely found in Brazil. It grows up to a height of 1.5–2 m and produces about 200–250 commercially usable leaves in a course of 6–7 years. It shows enhanced mechanical properties and as a result it is widely used in automotive industry, shipping industry, civil constructions, agricultural twine, etc. (Sanjay et al. 2018).

1.2.9 DATE PALM (*PHOENIX DACTYLIFERA*)

It is extensively grown for its fruit. It comprises approximately 19 species with more than 5000 cultivators all around the globe. These trees are the tallest among the Phoenix species (around 23 m high) (Alotaibi et al. 2019). The date palm rachis and its leaves are stored in greater quantity after the date farm fruits are harvested every year in different countries. It contains more cellulosic fiber and can be used as reinforcement in the matrix of polymers (Thermoplastic and Thermoset). It can be used in the automotive industry as well.

1.2.10 COCONUT FIBER (*COCOS NUCIFERA*)

It is obtained from the husk of a coconut fruit. It is the thickest fiber among all natural fibers. Coconut trees are grown in tropical regions, and the major producers of coconut fibers are India, Sri Lanka, Indonesia, Philippines and Malaysia. It has high amounts of lignin, lower cellulose and hemicellulose compared to other natural fibers. These fibers show excellent properties in terms of strength, resilience, damping, higher elongation, and resistance to wear and weather (Pham 2016). It is used for making ropes, mats, mattresses and brushes, in addition to its use in upholstery, agriculture and construction industries.

1.2.11 KAPOK (*CEIBA PENTANDRA*)

It belongs to the Bombacaceae family and grows in tropical regions. The fibers of this plant include silk cotton that is yellowish or light brown in color, which encloses the kapok seed. These fibers are lightweight, hydrophobic and cellulosic in nature (Prachayawarakorn et al. 2013) and are used for buoyancy, oil absorption, reinforcement, adsorption and biofuels.

1.2.12 BAMBOO (*BAMBUSOIDEAE*)

Bamboo is also known as the natural glass fiber because of its alignment in a longitudinal direction. It is extensively available in dense forests and in China. It is used as reinforcement in polymer matrix because of its low cost, high strength, lightweight and stiffness (Wang and Chen 2016). It has been traditionally used for building houses, bridges, boats, etc.

Sustainable Composites 7

1.2.13 SILK (*BOMBYX MORI*)

It is a fiber that is extracted from silkworms and has been used for making clothes since ancient times. It is largely found in China, South Asia and Europe. The larvae of Cocoons insects are used for fiber extraction (Das and Natarajan 2019). These fibers show excellent mechanical properties such as compressibility, extensibility and high strength.

1.2.14 COTTON (*GOSSIPIYUM*)

It belongs to the Hibisceae sub-tribe and the Malvaceae family. Cotton is the most commonly used fiber for making cloths. It is found in the tropical and subtropical regions of China, India and USA (Colomban and Jauzein 2018). Upland cotton and pima cotton are the most popular types of cottons. The cotton leaves are removed and collected and are then compressed into truckload-size modules. These modules are then transported to the cotton gin for processing. The gin separates the sticks, burrs and seeds from the cotton fibers. This method is widely used in textile industries, and presently researchers are working toward the development of such composites for industrial applications.

Figure 1.3 shows the appearance of different natural fibers.

1.3 PROPERTIES OF NATURAL FIBERS

Researchers are showing increasing interest in developing a new material with excellent mechanical properties as well as tribological properties for a wide range of applications, including those in the automotive, construction and biomedical industries. They have replaced the monolithic materials from fibers and materials such as aramid fibers, glass fibers and carbon fibers. But, these materials have a few disadvantages such as non-biodegradability, high energy consumption and threat to our environment. Hence, to overcome these issues, researchers have made an attempt to investigate the various properties of natural fiber reinforced composites. These composites show better mechanical properties and can replace synthetic fibers in many applications. The mechanical and physical properties with chemical composition of various natural fibers are shown in Table 1.1. The chemical structure of cellulose, hemicellulose and lignin is shown in Figure 1.4. Each structure consists of the –OH group. The presence of the –OH group in all natural fibers helps in the development of a strong interfacial bond between fibers and polymer (Nurazzi et al. 2021).

1.4 ADVANTAGES OF NATURAL FIBER COMPOSITES

Natural fibers as reinforcement in composite materials exhibit many advantages over other reinforced composite materials (Jawaid and Khalil 2011, Sanjay and Siengchin 2018).

FIGURE 1.3 Appearance of various types of natural fibers. (Rajak et al. 2019)

1. They show good mechanical properties, which can be improved further by chemical treatment.
2. They are renewable, fully biodegradable and environment friendly. Further, thermal recycling is possible.
3. They are cheap and easily available.
4. The weight of the composite is less than the synthetic based fibers.
5. When natural fiber-reinforced plastics are combusted once their life cycle is over, the amount of CO_2 released from the combustion process is equal to the amount assimilated during their growth.

Sustainable Composites

TABLE 1.1
Mechanical and Physical Properties with Chemical Composition of Various Natural Fibers

Fiber	Elastic Modulus (GPa)	Tensile Strength (MPa)	Elongation (%)	Density (g/cm³)	Chemical Composition (%)		
					Cellulose	Hemicellulose	Lignin
Jute	37.5–55	325–770	2.5	1.23–1.4	45–53	18–21	21–26
Flax	60–70	700–1000	2.3	1.38–1.4	64.1–71.9	64.1–71.9	2.0–2.2
Hemp	45	530–1110	2–4	1.35–1.47	70.2–74.4	17.9–22.4	3.7–5.7
Ramie	23	915	3.7	1.44–1.47	68.6–76.2	13.1–16.7	0.6–0.7
Banana	29	721–910	2	1.2–1.35	64	19	5
Bagasse	17	290	1.1	1.2–1.3	45–55	20–25	18–24
Henequen	13.2	500	4.8	1.4	-	-	-
Pineapple	11	188–308	0.8–1.2	1.2–1.5	68.5	18.8	6.04
Kenaf	41	745–930	1.6	1.2–1.45	45–57	8–13	21.5
Coir	6	140–175	27.5	1.2	30.58	26.7	33.3
Sisal	15.5	460–855	8	1.2–1.5	78	10	8
Abaca	41	410–810	3.4	1.5	56–63	20–25	7–9
Cotton	6–10	250–500	3–10	1.21–1.6	42.45	71.56	20.50
Nettle	38	650	1.7	1.5	-	-	-
Kraft	40	1000	4.4	1.5	70	25	3–5
Bamboo	27–40	593	3.5	1.2–1.5	26–43	30	21–33
Kapok	3–5	100–1500	0.7	1.69	35	22	21.5
Phormium	26.5	250–310	0.9	1.2–1.4	92	2	4
Quill Feather	3–10	100–203	6.9	0.9	-	-	-
Wool	2.3–5	50–315	13.2–35	1.3	-	-	-
Harakeke	14–33	440–990	4.2–5.8	1.3	-	-	-
Sugar palm	0.5–3.37	15.5–290	5.7–28	1.29	47.74	5.6	37.8
Betel nut	1.3–2.6	120–166	22–24	0.2–0.4	53	33	7.2
Sugarcane bagasse	5.1–6.2	170–350	6.3–7.9	1.1–1.6	46	27	23
Oil palm	0.6–9	50–400	4–8	0.7–1.6	65	17.5	10.12
Curaua	63.7	543	1	1.4	70.7	21.1	11.1
Date Palm	5–12	170–275	5–10	0.92	46	18	20
Almond Leaves	4.4	126.6	2.2	1.07	38.47	28.82	29.54
Corn Husk	4.57	160.49	21.08	1.254	31–39	34–41	2–14
Piassava	1.07–4.59	134–143	7.8–21.9	1.4	28.6	25.8	45

Source: Nurazzi et al. 2021; Thyavihalli Girijappa et al. 2019; Khalid et al. 2021; Rajak et al. 2019.

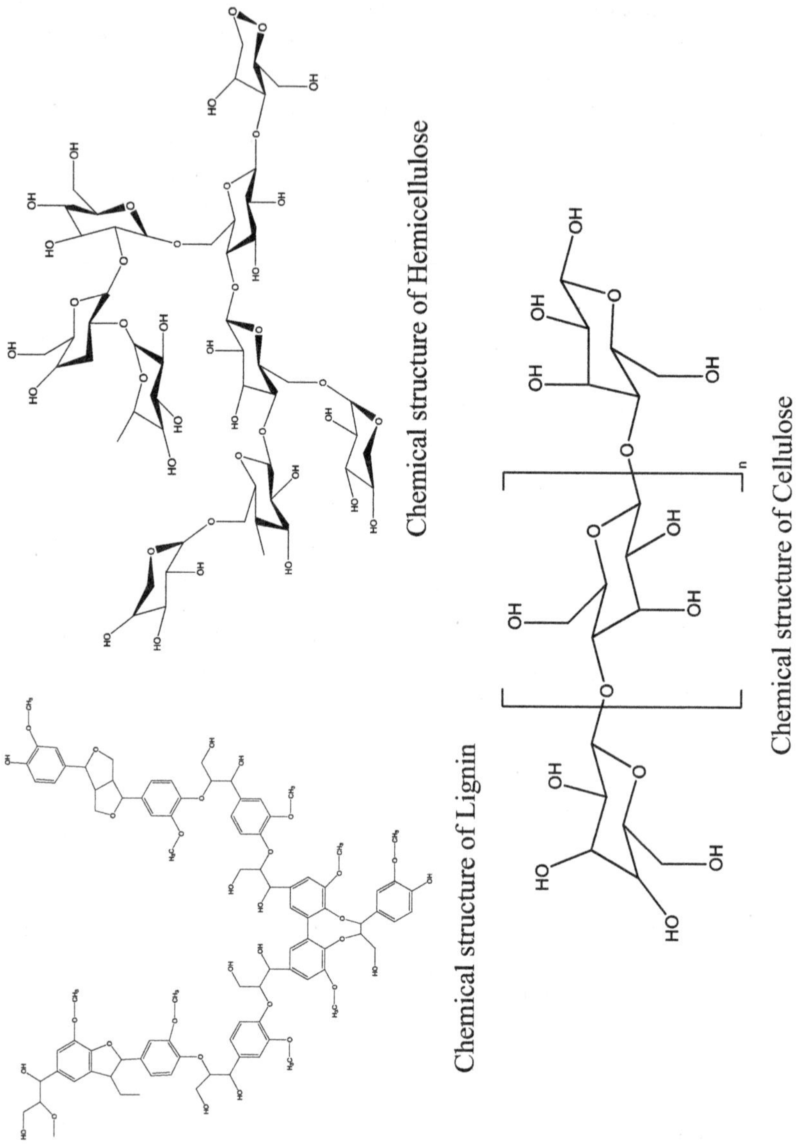

FIGURE 1.4 Chemical sturcture of lignin, hemicellulose and cellulose. (Nurazzi et al. 2021)

Sustainable Composites

1.5 DISADVANTAGES OF NATURAL FIBER COMPOSITES

1. The function of composite materials and their quality largely depend on the characteristic of natural fibers.
2. Natural fiber composites possess high moisture absorption reduced wettability.
3. They are incompatible with other matrices.
4. They show poor interfacial adhesion between the fiber and the matrix and have poor fire resistance.
5. They show lower impact strength.

1.6 EXTRACTION OF NATURAL FIBERS

The extraction of fibers from plants and animals is a major challenge. The most widely used methods to separate the fibers are water retting and dew retting. These methods require ~14–28 days for the degradation of cellulose, hemicellulose, lignin pectin and waxes that are present on the outer core of plants. It means these methods depend upon the category of fiber. Therefore, to overcome the problem of longer processing time, mechanical extraction and chemical treatment are performed. The comparison between extracting methods is given in Table 1.2.

1.7 FABRICATION TECHNIQUES

Natural fiber reinforced composites are developed by using polymer as a matrix. The polymer is categorized into four groups: linear polymer (chain molecules), thermosetting polymer (highly cross-linked molecules), thermoplastic polymer (molecules not interconnected) and elastomer (thermoplastic or lightly cross-linked thermosets having elastic deformation > 200%). The crosslinking of molecules in polymers occurs due to the polymerization process. The degree of polymerization is equal to the number of monomer units in the chain. Among all types of polymers, only thermosetting and thermoplastic polymers are widely used for the manufacturing of nanocomposites. The methods are summarized in Table 1.3.

Further, Table 1.4 presents the summarized data of the matrix materials used with natural fibers and their application. It also describes the manufacturing process for fabricating those composite materials. Furthermore, Table 1.5 shows the various matrixes available to develop the composite materials with respect to their application.

1.8 CHARACTERIZATION OF NATURAL FIBER COMPOSITES

This section provides an overview of the major characterization methods for natural fiber composites in previous published research by considering their morphological, physical, thermal and mechanical properties.

TABLE 1.2
Comparison Between Fibers Extraction Method

Extraction Methods	Dew Retting	Water Retting	Mechanical Extraction
Description	The gathered samples plant stems are spread evenly on the grassy fields: to receive a combined action of bacteria, sunlight, atmospheric air and dew that cause break down of its cellular tissues and adhesive substances that surrounds the fibers on the grassy fields; to receive a combined action of bacteria, sunlight, atmospheric air and dew that cause break down of its cellular tissues and adhesive substances that surrounds the fibers	Plant stems are submersed in water (rivers, ponds or tanks) and checked periodically (microbial retting)	Fibers hammering are separated with a hammer mill or/and decorticator
Duration	Two to three weeks, depending on the climatic conditions	7–14 days	Depending on production fibers
Advantages	Common in areas in locations having heavy night dew and warm day with limited water resources	The fibers produced are uniform and of higher quality	It produces large quantities of short fibers in a short time
Disadvantages	The obtained fibers are darker in color and are of poor quality. For dew retting process, the agricultural lands need to be occupied for several weeks, and also the obtained fibers are contaminated with soil and fungi.	High cost, environmental concerns and inferior fibers quality, but better than fibers obtained through dew retting process. Requires high water treatment maintenance	High cost and acceptable quality of fibers

Source: MR et al. 2019.

TABLE 1.3
Fabrication Process of Polymer Based Nanocomposite with Their Advantages, Disadvantages and Applications

Processes for the development of Thermosetting Matrix Nanocomposite

Methods	Process	Advantages	Disadvantages	Applications
Hand lay-up	Performed in open mold with the application of Gel coating followed by fiber layer.	Simple and easy, low tooling cost, large parts can be produced	Slow, Labor consuming job, Not good Quality and strength	Structural applications
Spray-up	Resin and chopped fibers are sprayed through two distinct sprays on open mold	Lower labor cost, design flexibility, low tooling cost	Slow, Labor consuming job, longer curing time, high waste factor	Caravan bodies, Truck fairings, Bathtubs, Small boats.
Filament Winding	Resin impregnated fibers are wound over a rotating mandrel at the desired angle.	Low scrap rate, formed non-cylindrical parts, flexible mandrel	Controls the filament tension, carefully chooses viscosity and pot life.	Pressure vessels, storage tanks and pipes, drive shafts, rocket motors, launch tubes
Pultrusion	Resin impregnated fibers are pulled from the heated die to make a part	Simple, low cost and high volume production process, good surface quality	Die jamming, fiber breakage, improper fiber wet-out	Electrical insulators, panels, beams, gratings, ladders
Pulforming	Similar process as Pultrusion with length formation in semicircular contour	Simple, low cost and high volume production process, good surface quality	Die jamming, fiber breakage, improper fiber wet-out	Curved cross-sections
Resin Transfer Molding (RTM)	Inserted Preformed and oriented reinforcement in the heated close mold die, then poured the resin and make the part	Large and curvature parts are easily made, less time used, high volume production process	Complex mold design, fiber may wash or move during resin transfer	Automobiles, aerospace, sporting goods and consumer products
Autoclave Molding	Closed vessel process under simultaneous application of high temperature and pressure	Less voids, excellent properties, cured many parts at same time	Expensive	Aerospace industry to fabricate high strength / weight ratio parts

(*continued*)

TABLE 1.3 (Continued)
Fabrication Process of Polymer Based Nanocomposite with Their Advantages, Disadvantages and Applications

Processes for the development of Thermosetting Matrix Nanocomposite

Methods	Process	Advantages	Disadvantages	Applications
Compression Molding	Heated thermosets are kept in lower die and the pressure through punch is applied to get the desired shape.	Low cost, fast setup time, molds heavy plastics	Lower production rate, rejected part cannot be reprocessed	Brush, mirror, handle, trays, cook-ware, automotive parts
Processes for Development of Thermoplastic Matrix Nanocomposite				
Injection Molding	Polymer and fiber mixture are melted and moved forward through reciprocating screw in mold cavity	Fully automated, Highly productive, highly accurate, easily fabricate complex shape parts	Higher tooling cost, limited length of fibers decreasing their reinforcing effect.	Boat hulls and lawn chairs, to bottle cups. Car parts, TV and computer housings
Diaphragm Forming	Insert thermopreg fabric in between heating and forming silicon sheets	Formed double curvature, easy fabrication		Engine cover, double curvature components
Automated Layup	Layers of prepreg (reinforcing phase impregnated by liquid resin) tape are applied on the mold surface by a tape application robot.	Low cost than hand lay-up	Limited to flat or low curvature.	Airframe components, bodies of boats, truck, tanks, swimming pools and ducts

Source: Katiyar and Sahu 2021.

Sustainable Composites

TABLE 1.4
Matrix Materials Used for Some Fibers with Their Applications and Manufacturing Techniques

Materials Used		Applications	Manufacturing Techniques
Fibers	**Matrix**	**Applications**	**Techniques**
Sisal	Polypropylene (PP), Polystyrene (PS), Epoxy Resin	Automobile body parts, roofing sheets	Hand lay-up, compression molding
Hemp	Polyethylene (PE), PP, Polyurethane (PU)	Furniture, automotive	RTM, compression molding
Kenaf	Polylactic acid (PLA), PP, epoxy resin	Tooling, bearings, automotive parts.	Compression molding, pultrusion
Flax	PP, polyester, epoxy	Structural, textile	Compression molding RTM, spray/hand lay-up, vacuum infusion
Ramie	PP, Polyolefin, PLA	Bulletproof vests, socket prosthesis, civil.	Extrusion with injection molding
Rice Husk	PU, PE	Window/door frames, automotive structure.	Compression/injection molding
Jute	Polyester, PP	Ropes, roofing, door panels.	Hand lay-up, compression/ injection molding
Coir	PP, epoxy resin, PE	Automobile structural components, building boards, roofing sheets, insulation boards.	Extrusion, injection molding

Source: Rajak et al. 2019.

TABLE 1.5
Various Matrixes and Their Properties and Applications

Matrix Material	Properties	Applications
Polyethersulfone	Flame resistant	Automotive
Polyphenylene sulfide	Resistance to chemicals and high temperature	Electrical
Polysulfone	Low moisture absorption, high strength, low creep	Marine, food packaging
Polyethylene (PE)	Resistance to corrosion	Piping

(continued)

16   Tribology in Sustainable Composites

TABLE 1.5 (Continued)
Various Matrixes and Their Properties and Applications

Matrix Material	Properties	Applications
Polypropylene (PP)	Resistance to chemicals	Packaging, automotive, construction
Polylactic acid (PLA)	Biodegradable, non-toxic	Food handling, bio-medical
Polyurethane (PU)	Wear resistance, low cost, sound and water-proof	Structural, acoustic
Poly(butylene adipate-co-terephthalate)-PBAT	Biodegradable, high stiffness	Coating, packaging
Poly(vinyl) alcohol	High tensile strength	Bio-medical
Natural rubber	Low density, low cost, biodegradable	Structural, automobile
Epoxy resin	High strength	Automotive, aerospace, marine
Polyester	Durable, resistance to water, chemicals	Structural

Source: Rajak et al. 2019.

1.8.1 MORPHOLOGICAL OBSERVATION

It is observed that the geometry and type of fiber, matrix, additives and fabrication processes significantly affect the behavior of natural composite materials. Further, any geometrical irregularities in fibers lower the strength because of weaker interface, poor compatibility and wetting between the polar fibers and non-polar polymer matrix. Moreover, to achieve the desired properties, it is crucial to optimize the fiber concentration in matrix. The higher the concentration of fibers in the matrix the higher the agglomeration of fibers, causing poor dispersion and formation of excessive cavities. This problem can be addressed with the help of a coupling agent (Nassar et al. 2021). Therefore, morphological analysis in fiber composites plays a significant role in identifying homogeneous distribution, voids/cavity, etc. Morphological analysis can be done using optical microscopy and scanning electron microscopy (SEM). Using the analysis it was observed that the interfacial bonding can occur in four different forms: (a) mechanical interlocking, (b) chemical bonding, (c) molecular inter diffusion and (d) electrostatic bonding (shown in Figure 1.5).

1.8.2 PHYSICAL PROPERTIES

Different physical properties in natural fiber composites need to be investigated, such as water absorption test, crystallinity test and density. It is noted that sustainable composites have less density in comparison to other composites, which is based on

Sustainable Composites 17

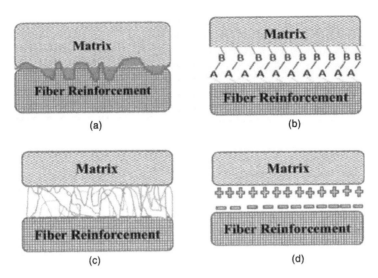

FIGURE 1.5 Various forms of interfacial bonding between matrix and fiber: (a) mechanical interlocking, (b) chemical bonding, (c) molecular inter diffusion and (d) electrostatic bonding. (Nassar et al. 2021)

the strength of internal bond. The bond strength increases with increase in density. Another physical property that needs to be identified is crystallinity, which is characterized by atomic, ionic or molecular order, crystallographic planes and the number of amorphous phases. To analyze this property of fiber composites, X-ray diffraction (XRD) is used.

Water absorption is the most important physical property test. In natural fibers reinforced composites, water penetrates deeper due to the presence of lumens and hydroxyl groups, which makes the composite surface hydrophilic in nature. Additionally, water absorption in fiber composites occurs through fine voids, gaps between the polymer and the fiber, and micro-cracks in the polymeric matrix (Nassar et al. 2021). Therefore, the polymer–filler interfacial strength significantly affects the water uptake of the eco-composites, as illustrated in Figure 1.6. This can be controlled by the optimum concentration of fibers in the matrix.

1.8.3 Thermal Behavior

The thermal behavior of composite materials is investigated using thermogravimetric analyzer and differential scanning calorimetry (DSC). It is an essential property of composite as it affects the mechanical properties significantly. It is observed that different plant fibers show a range of temperature variations due to the presence of lignin, hemicellulose, cellulose and pectin in plants. Most of the fibers start degrading at 220°C, which can be corrected by removing excessive amounts of lignin, hemicellulose and other alkaline soluble substances using physical, chemical or biological treatment of fibers (Nassar et al. 2021).

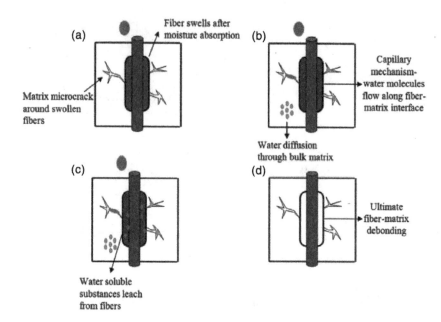

FIGURE 1.6 Mechanism of water diffusion in eco-composites. (Nassar et al. 2021)

1.8.4 Mechanical Performance

The mechanical properties depend on the types of polymer or fiber used in the fabrication of composite materials. Further, the way the composite material is processed also affects its mechanical performance. For structural application of composite material, mechanical properties hold importance. There are different mechanical evaluations conducted on a material and some are very specific to an individual application. However, the general focus of most researchers is on a few tests including tensile test, flexural test, impact test, compression test and hardness. These few tests can reveal the mechanical behavior of composite materials to a large extent and also give an insight to other possible areas of applications (Shesan et al. 2019).

1.8.4.1 Tensile Test

It involves one of the most fundamental and commonly used mechanical testing of polymeric materials using universal testing machines. This test is used to determine the stress–strain behavior under tension. In this test, tensile force (pulling force) is applied to a composite material, and the response of the specimens to that applied force (stress) is measured. The samples are subjected to controlled tension until failure. This test determines the strength of the material and its capability to elongation. From this test, some highly desired properties such as Young's modulus, yield strength, percentage elongation and ultimate tensile strength (UTS) can be derived.

Sustainable Composites

1.8.4.2 Flexural Test

The purpose of this test is to assess whether a material is able to resist bending forces applied directly perpendicular to its longitudinal axis with the use of three-point or four-point bend testing. It is also known as a transverse beam test. Flexural properties are among the most important parameters for assessing the suitability of composite materials for structural applications. Flexural load, flexural Young's modulus, flexural strength and deflection at break are measured and used to interpret the mechanical behavior under flexural stress.

1.8.4.3 Impact Test

It is employed for assessing the impact strength, toughness and notch sensitivity of structural materials using the Izod or the Charpy test method. In summary, this test determines the capability of the material to withstand high rate loading. Further, the impact test is very critical for most polymer materials because it relates to the product performance and service life. It also influences other properties related to product safety and liability.

1.8.4.4 Compressive Strength

This test is done to evaluate the material behavior when subjected to uniaxial compression load at a relatively low and uniform loading rate using a universal testing machine. It is an essential component of product design analysis, especially materials for building purposes. Compressive strength and compressive Young's modulus are the two major properties that are used in construction industry. However, compressive strain, deformation beyond yield point and compressive yield stress are evaluated through the same test.

1.8.4.5 Hardness Test

Hardness is the property of a material that enables it to resist scratching, indentation, penetration and plastic deformation. Hardness, therefore, in any structural material is important from engineering point of view, as it improves the resistance to wear due to erosion or corrosion. The shore D hardness test is generally carried out to obtain the hardness of the material.

1.8.4.6 Crashworthiness

A crashworthiness test determines how well a vehicle or aircraft will protect its occupants in case of an accident. It is most important concept to identify any vehicle defect. As a result, it can have the ability to prevent injuries to the occupant during collision. Therefore, crashworthiness focuses on occupant protection to reduce fatality during accidents. Different criteria can be used to determine crashworthiness depending on the nature of the impact and vehicle involved. In general, the properties of composites materials depend on factors such as fiber length, fiber weight percentage content and the extent of polymer/fiber interactions.

1.8.5 Tribological Performance

Tribology is a subject that deals with friction, wear and lubrication. It helps in better understanding of wear and friction with lubrication. Even though various research works have been performed to observe the behavior of materials, the term 'tribology' was coined in 1960s after Jost's report. Further, an appropriate understanding of tribology and its concepts will save substantial money in maintenance costs. Certain studies indicate that the tribology activity of natural fiber-based composite is not the same because it relies heavily on manufacturing concepts such as operational parameters, physical and interfacial adhesion features, fiber additives and touch conditions. The various types of tribometers used to analyze the tribological behavior of sustainable composites according to the application are shown in Table 1.6.

TABLE 1.6
Tribo-Testing Equipment

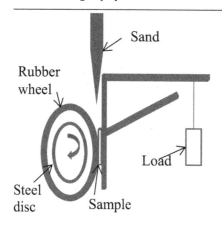

(i) **Rubber wheel test**
1. Dry Sand Rubber Wheel (DSRW) follows ASTM-G65
2. Wet Sand Rubber Wheel (WSRW) follows ASTM-G105
3. Sand/Steel wheel (SSW) test in wet/dry conditions follows ASTM- B 611
   - Abrasive wear behavior of materials under three-body conditions.
   - Dimension of the specimen is 70mm x 20mm x 7mm
   - The rubber wheel get in touch with the specimen under a load
   - Silica sand particles (i.e. fine, grain or coarse) are then introduced between the specimen and a rotating rubber wheel
   - Used also for adhesive testing
   - Operating parameters: applied load, rubber hardness, sliding speed.
   - Applications: tires, bushes, bearings and rollers

Sustainable Composites

TABLE 1.6 (Continued)
Tribo-Testing Equipment

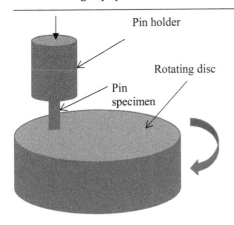

Pin-on-disc abrasion test

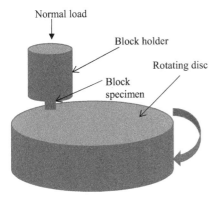

Block on disc test

(ii) **Pin-on-disk test**
- Pin-on-disc abrasion test follows ASTM G99-05
- Dimension of the specimen is 10mm x 10mm 20mm.
- The test specimen is set perpendicular under loading against rotating counterface.
- Contact area is not varying with respect to sliding time.
- Operating parameters: sliding velocity, sliding distance, normal load, wet or dry sliding, abrasive or adhesive contact condition.
- Application: sliding wear of various materials where constant contact area of interest.

(iii) **Block on disc test**
- Block on Disc Test follows ASTMG99
- Dimension of the specimen is 10mm x 10mm x 20mm.
- The test specimen is placed vertically to the counterface, which is rotating.
- An infrared thermometer can be used for the measuring interfaces temperatures during the interaction of sample and counterface.
- Contact area is not varying with respect to sliding time.
- Test can be adhesive and abrasive.
- Operating parameters: sliding velocity, sliding distance, normal load, wet or dry sliding, abrasive or adhesive contact condition.
- Applications: sliding wear of various materials where constant contact area of interest.

(*continued*)

TABLE 1.6 (Continued)
Tribo-Testing Equipment

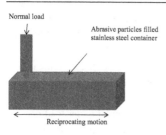

Linear Reciprocating Abrasion Testing

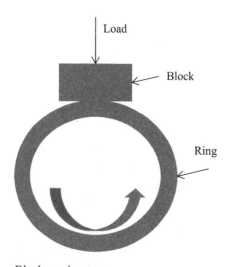

Block on ring test

(iv) **Linear reciprocating test**
- Linear reciprocating abrasion test follows ASTM G133-05e1.
- Abrasive wear behavior of materials under three-body conditions.
- It has space for a variety of sample geometries to form point, line and area contacts.
- Stainless steel container filled with abrasive moves linearly with the help of the power screw, which is directly coupled to the motor and the specimen slides in the abrasive particles filled container.
- Test is abrasive in the presence of abrasive particles in the stainless steel container, otherwise the test is purely adhesive
- Operating parameters: sliding velocity, wet or dry sliding, abrasive types, applied load
- Application: linear sliding of window panels, door handles, lock mechanisms

(v) **Block on ring test**
- Block on Ring Test follows ASTM G77, G137-95 standards.
- Dimension of the specimen is 10mm x 20mm x 50mm.
- Test sample place parallel to the side of the counterface and contact surface varies with the sliding time.
- Operating parameter: sliding velocity, sliding distance, applied load, temperature, wet or dry sliding
- Applications: crankshafts, camshafts, piston pins, connecting rods, suspensions, lubricants

Sustainable Composites

TABLE 1.6 (Continued)
Tribo-Testing Equipment

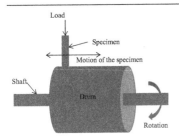

Pin on drum test

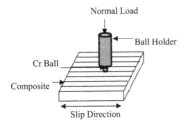

Low-amplitude oscillating Test

(vi) **Pin on drum test**
- Pin on drum test follows ASTM A514
- Specimen travels linearly which is placed horizontally against a rotating drum.
- The drum is covered with abrasive paper. Without abrasive paper, test is simply adhesive.
- Operating parameters: sliding distance, sliding velocity, applied load, wet or dry sliding, abrasive or adhesive contact condition.
- Applications: conveyor belts, rotating rollers etc.

(vii) **Low-amplitude oscillating test**
- Known as Fretting wear
- 10 mm x10 mm x 3–4 mm
- A polished chromium steel ball of having surface roughness values in the range 0.01–0.015 µm oscillates against the specimen. The diameter of the ball is 10 mm.
- Operating parameter: Load, sliding velocity, number of cycles, slip amplitude, slip, frequency, contact geometry, material properties, environment.
- Application: Bearings, gears, bushes, flanges, multilayer leaf springs, palliatives

(*continued*)

TABLE 1.6 (Continued)
Tribo-Testing Equipment

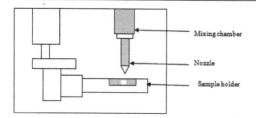

(viii) **Erosion test**
- Erosion test follows ASTM: G76–07
- Dimension of the specimen 20mm×20mm
- The dry and compressed air with the solid sand particles hit on the test sample at various speeds and angle at constant feed rate through converging nozzle.
- Stand of distance is 10 mm.
- Operating parameters: impingement angle, impact velocity, erodent type
- Application: rotor blade, conveyer belt

Source: Katiyar and Jena 2022.

1.9 POSSIBILITIES TO IMPROVE THE PROPERTIES OF NATURAL FIBERS

It is observed in many research works that natural fiber reinforced composites show poor interfacial bonding between fiber and matrix due to hydrophilic nature, poor wettability, moisture absorption and water absorption. Further, treatment of fibers through physical or chemical means should ideally be performed before their use in the matrix.

1.9.1 Physical Treatment

This process does not affect strongly the chemical composition of fibers. Stretching of fibers, calendar therapy of fibers, corona, thermal and plasma treatment of fibers, and the mechanical interface of polymers are involved in the process. Greater mechanical bond between fiber and matrix generally improves the interface strength. Fine threads of natural fibers are derived using yarning techniques. Various reports state that the physical approach modifies the surface of natural fibers, which is a shallow treatment of the cell wall and does not affect the fiber's hygroscopic properties. Physical therapy definitely enhances resilience, elongation and modulation, but extensive physical therapy damages the fibers. As a result chemical treatments are used to improve the fiber properties (Nurazzi et al. 2021).

Sustainable Composites

1.9.2 CHEMICAL TREATMENT

Presently, researchers have growing interest to develop the newer materials using natural fibers reinforced composites as an alternate to carbon/glass reinforced composites in various application such as automobile interior, pedestrian bridge, shipping pallets, composite roof tiles, furniture and toys (Khalid et al. 2021). But, the main disadvantage of natural fiber is poor interaction of fiber and matrix, hydrophilic nature due to which natural fiber reinforced composites show poor mechanical properties. Therefore, modifying the fibers through chemical treatment is required make them less hydrophilic. The various chemical treatments are described below.

1.9.2.1 Alkaline Treatment

It is well known that the fiber entails pectin, waxy materials, lignin and oil that are covered by the outer layer of the fiber cell. The fiber structure is altered by chemical treatment using sodium hydroxide (NaOH) as a reagent. It alters the cellulose structure by cleaning the surfaces. This process is known as alkalization. Researchers have treated hemp, kenaf, jute, sisal and kapok fibers with the NaOH at 20°C for about 48 h. Further, the fibers are washed using distilled water followed by acetic acid to neutralize the excess of NaOH. The treated fibers showed excellent interfacial adhesion between fiber and matrix, resulting in the improvement of mechanical and thermal properties of the composite materials. Using retting process, the extracted fibers from Napier grass are treated with 2–5% concentration of NaOH solution at room temperature for a duration of 30 min. The fibers are cleaned by distilled water that removes the hemicellulose and then dried at 100 °C. The alkaline treatment reduces the hemicellulose in the fiber, resulting in enhanced mechanical properties when compared to untreated fibers. It can be concluded from various research works that researchers have varied the NaOH concentration from 2% to 5% for 15–60 minutes at room temperature followed by distilled water washing and experimenting at higher temperature for longer durations in alkalization process (Saravanakumaar et al. 2018; Asumani et al. 2012).

1.9.2.2 Silane Treatment

In this treatment, silane is added with NaOH to treat the fiber and matrix interface. It forms the silanol groups (Si-OH) that form strong bonds with the –OH groups of the fibers, due to which the strength of fiber composite is improved. This process is used to treat the sugar palm fibers. These fibers are treated with 2% silane and 6% NaOH for a duration of 3 h. The treated fibers showed the enhanced interfacial interaction between fiber and matrix. Further, some researchers have observed the mechanical properties of silane treated composites at different soaking times. They observed enhancement in strength due to the formation of silanol groups. Some silanol groups come strong with –OH groups of fibers and remaining silanol groups undergo condensation with the neighboring silanol groups. It can be concluded that the whole treatment forms the hydrophobic polymerized silane that can attach to matrix via van der Waals forces (Debeli et al. 2018; Atiqah et al. 2018).

1.9.2.3 Acetylation Treatment

In this process of acetylation, the acetyl group is formed on the fiber surface. It was used to decrease the hydrophilic nature of fibers with stability to the composites. It enhances the adhesion property between fiber and matrix, resulting in the formation of strong bond that provides excellent properties in composites. The acetyl group is reacted with the –OH group of fibers that makes the surface of fibers hydrophobic. Therefore, lignin and hemicellulose contained in fibers are treated by this process (Sreekala and Thomas 2003; Rong et al. 2001).

1.9.2.4 Peroxide Treatment

This treatment is generally applied on cellulose fibers for obtaining better mechanical properties of composites. By decomposition of peroxide, it forms free radicals, which react with the hydroxyl group of cellulose fiber and matrix. This process is performed after the alkalization of fibers. The alkaline treated fibers were dipped in 6% concentration of benzoyl peroxide or dicumyl peroxide in acetone for ~30 min (Li et al. 2007).

1.9.2.5 Benzoylation Treatment

In this method, the fibers are first treated with NaOH followed by benzoyl chloride (C_6H_5COCl) treatment for ~15min. After that, fibers are isolated and treated with ethanol for ~1 min followed by distilled water washing and then, drying of fibers in oven at 80 °C for 24 h. This improves the thermal stability of fibers in comparison to untreated fibers and reduces the hydrophilic nature of the fibers. Further, it makes the bond between fiber/matrix stronger, resulting in improved strength of the composites (Zhang et al. 2005).

1.9.2.6 Potassium Permanganate ($KMnO_4$) Treatment

It is applied after the alkaline treatment of fibers for enhancing the interfacial bond between fiber and matrix. It is carried out for a duration of 1–5 min with the $KMnO_4$ concentration of 0.005%–0.5% along with acetone. After that, the treated fibers are dried in an oven (Khan et al. 2006; Zaman et al. 2010).

1.9.2.7 Stearic Acid Treatment

Stearic acid treatment is performed to alkali-treated non-woven jute fibers in different concentrations of stearic acid (~1%) mixed in anhydrous ethanol for 1 min to 4 h depending upon the application. It is followed by drying at 80°C to 100°C for 45 min to 1 h (Paul et al. 1997).

Table 1.7 summarizes different chemical treatments for different natural fibers. Table 1.8 summarizes different chemical treatments with functional groups and their effect on fibers.

Table 1.9 summarizes the recent treatments of natural fiber reinforced bio-composites carried out by researchers, and Table 1.10 summarizes the comparison of tensile strength of treated and untreated natural fibers.

Sustainable Composites

27

TABLE 1.7

Use of Different Reagents in Treatment of Different Fibers

Fibers	Chemical Reagents Used
Pineapple Leaf	c-aminopropyl trimethoxy silane (Z-6011) and c-methacrylate propyl trimethoxy (Z-6030), NaOH and KOH
Green coconut	NaOCl, NaOCl/NaOH or H_2O_2
Alfa	NaOH
Carica Papaya	NaOH
Kenaf	NaOH
Hemp	(3-glycidyloxypropyl)trimrthoxysilane
Ramie	NaOH, NaOH/Saline, Silane
Sisal	Stearic acid
Okra Bast	$NaClO_2$
Flax	Methyl methacrylate

Source: Thyavihalli Girijappa et al. 2019.

TABLE 1.8

Different Chemical Treatment with Functional Groups and Their Specific Effects on Fibers

Chemical Treatment	Functional Groups/Coupling Agent	Effect on Natural Fibers
Benzoylation treatment	Benzoyl chloride	Fibers become hydrophobic
Peroxide treatment	Polyethylene	Enhances the adhesion between fiber and matrix
Sodium Chlorite treatment	$NaOClO_2$	Removes moisture from fibers
Acrylation and acrylonitrile grafting	Acrylic acid (CH_2= CHCOOH)	Bonding capacity and stress transfer of the interface enhances
Oleoyl Chloride treatment	Oleoyl chloride	Enhances wettability and adhesion properties
Triazine treatment	Triazine ($C_3H_3N_3$)	Improves the adhesion of fibers
Potassium Permanganate treatment	$KMnO_4$	Thermal stability of fibers enhances
Fungal treatment	Specific enzymes	Improves the linking/meshing of fibers in the matrix

Source: Khalid et al. 2021.

TABLE 1.9

Summary from the 2015–2020 Period on Recent Treatments of Natural Fiber Reinforced Bio-Composites

Type of Treatment	Natural Fiber	Matrix	Method	Performance	
				Thermal	**Mechanical**
Physical Treatment	Alfa	Poly(lactic) acid	Calendaring	----	Composite material improved 34% of Young's modulus
	Pineapple leaf fiber	Poly(lactic) acid	Plasma physical treatment	PLA/10% wt. S- PALF exhibited enhanced degree of crystallinity by 27% compared to virgin PLA	10% wt. PALF/PLA displayed improved tensile modulus and yield strength by 60% and 6%, respectively
	Rice husk	Poly(lactic) acid	Plasma surface treatment	By the 30% mass of NF and the highest cooling rate of 40°C/min, the PLA/RH degree of crystallinity improved by 4- fold	30% mass RH/PLA exhibited improved flexural modulus from 3541 to 4615 MPa
	Rice husk	Poly(lactic) acid	Ozone surface treatment	Degree of crystallinity of 30% mass RH/PLA improved by 400% relative to untreated one	30% mass RH/PLA exhibited improved flexural modulus from 3541 to 4747 MPa
	Flax fiber	Thermoplastic polyolefin	Corona surface treatment	---	Surface treatment induces an increase in elongation by 14% whereas decrease in tensile strength and Young's modulus for about −14% and −21%, respectively
	Bamboo powder	Poly(lactic) acid	Electron beam irradiation	Electron beam irradiated 5 wt.% BP/PLA showed small improvement of thermal stability as compared to neat PLA by 1%	PLA/EBP 5 wt.% possessed lower tensile strength and modulus for about −1% and −11%, respectively

	Fiber	Matrix	Treatment	Thermal	Mechanical
	Sugar palm yarn fiber	Unsaturated polyester	Yarning process	The increasing SPF decreased the thermal stability of the composite due to fiber-fiber interaction, by −13%	50 wt.% fiber loading contributed to decrease in tensile strength by almost 17%, enhanced its tensile modulus by 10%
Chemical Treatment	Alfa fiber	Poly(lactic) acid	0.4M NaOH alkaline treatment	---	The tensile strength and Young's modulus of treated 20 wt.% fiber loading improved by 17% and 45%, respectively
	Alfa fiber	Poly(lactic) acid	Xylanases enzymatic treatment	---	1% xylanase-treated composite exhibited improvements in tensile strength and Young's modulus by 26.5% and 49.9%, accordingly
	Alfa fiber	Poly(lactic) acid	Pectinases enzymatic treatment	---	
	Sugarcane bagasse fiber	Cardanol resin	5% NaOH Alkaline treatment	15 wt.% bagasse fiber obtained maximum thermal stability, enhanced from 300 to 450°C, by almost 50%	Treated 15 wt.% bagasse fiber exhibited improved neat polymer tensile and tensile modulus by 54% (from 28 MPa to 18.2 MPa) and 83% (from 2.2 GPa to 1.2 GPa), respectively
	Sugar Palm Fiber	Unsaturated polyester	Seawater Treatment	---	Treated 15 cm SPF reinforced polyester composite exhibited higher tensile strength than the untreated one by 16%, with tensile modulus 30% lower
	Sisal Fiber	Epoxy resin	12% NaOH alkali treatment	Loss modulus of epoxy reinforced with 1 wt.% alkali-treated sisal fibers enhanced from 82 °C to 93 °C.	Flexural stress of the epoxy filled 1 wt.% alkali-treated sisal fibers exhibited improvement, from 83 MPa to 110 MPa

(continued)

TABLE 1.9 (Continued)
Summary from the 2015–2020 Period on Recent Treatments of Natural Fiber Reinforced Bio-Composites

Type of Treatment	Natural Fiber	Matrix	Method	Performance	
				Thermal	**Mechanical**
	Jute and coir fibers	Poly(lactic) acid	5% NaOH + KH560 alkali treatment	Combined treated jute-coir fibers reinforced PLA biocomposites had improved its thermal stability, which is 9.21% higher compared to pure PLA.	40:60 fibre:PLA ratio has enhanced tensile strength and modulus by 116% and 67%, respectively
	Water hyacinth fibers	Bioepoxy resin	5% solution of NaOH alkali treatment	Slightly same	WHF/epoxy exhibited enhanced tensile modulus, from 1868.9 MPa to 2105.8 MPa
	Water hyacinth fibers	Bioepoxy resin	1% solution of (3-Aminopropyl) triethoxysilane silane treatment	After silane treatment, WHFs start to decompose at 329.71°C is the highest increasing around 12% comparing with raw WHFs	Tensile modulus and strength of WHF/epoxy improved, by 1.1% and 15.7%, respectively
	Roselle fiber	Vinyl ester	9% NaOH alkali treatment	Thermal stability of fiber/vinyl ester had improved 6%	Tensile strength of the composite improved by 33.3%, from 15 MPa to 20 MPa
	Roselle fiber	Vinyl ester	Silane treatment	No slight improvement	Improved tensile strength from 15 MPa to 25 MPa, 66.7%
	Sugar Palm Fibers	Polyurethane	6% NaOH alkali treatment	---	Tensile strength improved by 18%
	Sugar Palm Fibers	Polyurethane	2% silane treatment	---	Tensile strength enhanced by 30%

Source: Nurazzi et al. 2021.

Sustainable Composites 31

TABLE 1.10
Effect of Various Treatment Methods on the Tensile Strength of Natural Fibers

| Fiber Type | Treatment Procedure | S_{UT} (MPa) | |
		Untreated	Treated
Date Palm Pedicles	Ethanol/Water; Acidified Sodium Chloride; NaOH	80	444
Date Palm Rachis	2% NaOH	174.2	242.6
Date Palm Mesh	1% NaOH	176	310
Abaca	5% NaOH	755	847
Banana	5% NaOH	780.3	536.2
Coconut	20% NaOH	186.4	280.9
Flax	5% NaOH	630	627
Husk	5% NaOH	108.8	135.2
Husk	Alkali-KH570	108.8	154.9
Sisal	2% NaOH	283.5	381.5
Sugarcane	5% NaOH	169.5	204.5

Source: Nassar et al. 2021.

1.9.2.8 Functionalization of Polymers and Natural Fibers

In many research works, it was noticed that the adhesion between fibers and polymers improves either by chemical treatment or physical treatment processes. But, surface modifications of fibers or polymers or both can also improve the mechanical interlocking. Natural fibers are used in polar group because of the presence of –OH group on the surface. This –OH group is due to the presence of cellulose molecule in natural fibers. It can be used to develop the more reactive chemical bonding. Further, polymer functionalization is carried out with the help of compatibilizers and coupling agents using different methods to fabricate high performance sustainable composites. It is reported that the combination of chemical treatment of fibers and irradiation of the polymer develop the composites with improved compatibility compared to chemical treatment. These composites exhibited improved mechanical properties, high thermal stability and reduced water absorption property (Martins et al. 2016; Anbupalani et al. 2020).

Moreover, low surface energy and lack of polar groups are reported for common polymer resin in many researches due to which it shows insufficient adhesion properties. Therefore, coupling agents are used to develop excellent adhesion between fibers and polymer. These coupling agents may be either reactive or non-reactive and may encourage compatibility. Hence, functionalization of fibers or polymers is important to improve the interfacial adhesion. In polymer, it can be carried out either in a solid phase or melt phase in the presence of coupling agents and an initiator. Figure 1.7 shows the possible techniques to modify the polymer surface. Moreover, the surface modification of natural fibers is carried out by

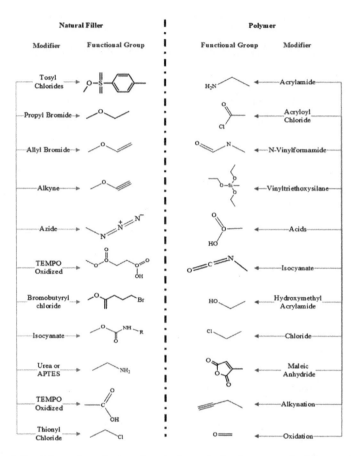

FIGURE 1.7 Schematic of the chemical methods for natural filler and polymer functionalization. (Nassar et al. 2021)

chemical treatment followed by cleaning. It exposes the –OH groups at surface of natural fibers. The presence of –OH group at fiber surface with various reactive coupling agents helps in the development of bond between fiber and polymer and improves the hydrophobicity of composites. Generally, functionalization of fibers (fillers) is carried out chemically prior to mixing (Nassar et al. 2021). Figure 1.7 (left column) shows the possible techniques of chemical processing of natural fibers (fillers).

Due to the chemical reaction, the intermolecular crosslinking and bonding is initiated between fiber and polymer. Therefore, it is noticed that the enhancement in properties of sustainable composites usually depend on the fiber surface and the type of chemical bond, which can be achieved by proper selection of surface modification of fibers and polymer, as shown in Figure 1.7. The strong bonding between fibers and polymers improves the mechanical properties, load transfer property and reduces water absorption. Figure 1.8 shows two examples of chemical crosslinking of fiber/

Sustainable Composites

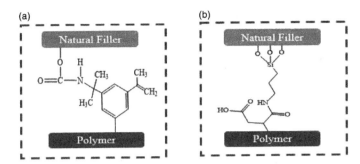

FIGURE 1.8 Chemical crosslinking between fibers (fillers) and polymer: (a) filler and functionalized polymer, (b) functionalized filler and functionalized polymer. (Nassar et al. 2021)

polymer composites. In Figure 1.8 (a), a reactive group is developed at polymer surface using functionalization. It reacts with –OH group of fibers. In this case, prior treatment of natural fiber is recommended due to which fiber surface is exposed to –OH groups (Willberg-Keyriläinen et al. 2018).

Further, researchers have developed similar and novel techniques, which are not used in general to functionalize the polymer. It is carried out using isocyanate group. This group is highly reactive with –OH group and makes the urethane bond between fibers and polymer that is very strong bond.

1.10 FACTORS AFFECTING THE PERFORMANCE OF NATURAL FIBERS REINFORCED COMPOSITES (NFRCs)

There are various factors affecting the performance of natural fibers reinforced composite materials. These are presented using fish bone diagrams (Figure 1.9), and are described as follows (Nurazzi et al. 2021; Chaudhary et al. 2018).

1. **Type of Fiber:** It plays a very significant role in the mechanical and tribological performance of NFRCs. It includes the length of fiber and its chemical composition. Further, it is also includes treated or untreated fibers that is more influenced in the properties of NFRCs.
2. **Type of Polymer:** It includes thermoplastic, thermoset and elastomer. In most of the cases, thermoset is used as matrix due to its excellent mechanical property and ability to work at higher temperature than thermoplastic. Therefore, it is important to select the proper polymer to fabricate the composites.
3. **Interfacial adhesion between fiber and matrix:** Proper physical or chemical treatment is required to obtain the significant interfacial adhesion strength between fiber and matrix.
4. **Effect of fiber orientation:** It refers to the random, unidirectional, bidirectional and parallel orientation of the fiber. The best mechanical

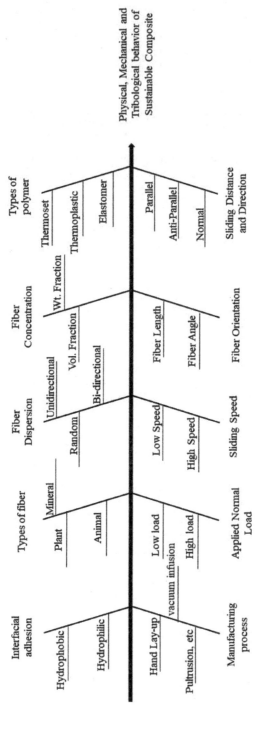

FIGURE 1.9 Representation of factors affecting the performance of NFRCs using the fishbone diagram.

Sustainable Composites 35

properties are generally obtained when a fiber is oriented parallel to the method of loading unit.

5. **Effect of fiber loading:** It means the concentration of fibers in the matrix either by weight or by volume. To achieve the desired properties, it is essential to optimize the fiber concentration in the matrix. Higher concentration of fibers in matrix results in the agglomeration of fibers, causing poor dispersion and formation of excessive cavities.

6. **Chemical composition of fibers:** The types of fibers are usually classified by their origin: plants, animal or mineral. Cellulose is the principal structural element of all plant fibers, while protein is specifically observed in animal fibers.

7. **Manufacturing process:** The mechanical performance of natural fibers affects the processing of natural fibers to a great extent. Therefore, it is necessary to select a proper manufacturing process to develop composite materials.

8. **Sliding Speed:** It depends upon the properties of fiber and polymer. Therefore, with increase in sliding speed, the tribological properties (friction and wear) may increase or decrease. Further, it is observed that increasing of sliding speed increases the interfacial temperature.

9. **Sliding Distance:** It is another important parameter that affects the tribological performance of NFRCs. It is observed that increasing of sliding distance friction coefficient helps in attaining the steady state condition but increases the wear loss of NFRCs. The effects are normally predictable for NFRCs and as a result in many investigations it is kept constant.

10. **Sliding Direction:** Based on the direction, there are three orientations used in tribo testing: parallel, anti-parallel and normal. It was observed that anti-parallel shows better wear performance compared to other orientations. This is due to more resistance provided by fibers.

1.11 APPLICATIONS OF NATURAL FIBERS

Fibers are usually classified in three categories similar to conventional end uses, such as clothing, household products and vehicles. Fashion applications used linseed, hemp and some amount of kapok with cotton fiber. Further, for household applications seed fiber, leaf fiber and bast fiber with the exception of bamboo fiber are used for making of tissues, mattresses, quilts etc. The potential applications of natural fibers composites are described in Table 1.11.

1.12 SUSTAINABILITY OF NATURAL FIBER REINFORCED COMPOSITES (NFRCs)

Because of the renewable and biodegradable nature of natural fibers, these are considered as emerging materials in many applications in the 21st century. It makes them environment friendly or ecofriendly (Adeyi et al. 2021).Since governments continue to raise guidelines against non-renewable and non-biodegradable materials, such materials are becoming increasingly popular around the world. The researchers have also encouraged the development of biomaterials specially NFRCs. To fabricate

TABLE 1.11
Potential Applications of Natural Fiber Composites

Fiber materials	Applications
Bast fibers	Instruments panels, covers, supports for hard and soft sets of guns, panels for sear back, panels of screens, headliners, walls of the side and back, benches of the back, bases, central consoles, load floors, trunk of trimmings
Abaca	Panels and body panels beneath the floor
Banana	Packaging paper
Coconut	Chair floors, headrest and back coils, interior trim and seat coiling, sitting surfaces
Coir	Seat coverings for buses, mattresses, doormats, rugs, bags, trays, packaging
Cotton	Sound insulation, panel trunk, insulation
Fiber wood recycled	Plastic retainer for panels of seat back
Flax	Setbacks and rear floor panels, floor panels, center consoles and pavement panels, Green wall panels. Other interior trim.
Hemp	Gate panel carriers, racing motorcycles, musical instruments
Sisal	Window panels and door linings, door panels
Kenaf	External door box, cell phone casing
Wood	Carrier for door frames, capped instrument pans, capped inserts and materials, capped seat back panels, fiber for cushions, fittings, pneumatic repair, cover, mobile house building
Wool	Upholstery, seat coverings

Source: Peças et al. 2018.

these materials, natural fibers play a vital role. Further, lower energy (9.55 MJ/kg) is consumed in the development of NFRCs in comparison to traditional composites, such as glass fiber reinforced composites (54.7 MJ/kg) (Joshi et al. 2004). Furthermore, natural fibers have the significant benefit in terms of revenue from their cultivation, which is due to the fact that land can be used to cultivate natural fibers multiple times, e.g., the flax and hemp cultivation further yields seeds, substances and oils with various critical uses for individuals, including health supplements. Some common elements that correlate with sustainable NFRCs materials are shown in Figure 1.10.

1.12.1 ENVIRONMENTAL PERSPECTIVE

As per the different life cycle assessment research, it was observed that the composites materials have shown better results over the conventional aluminum structures

Sustainable Composites

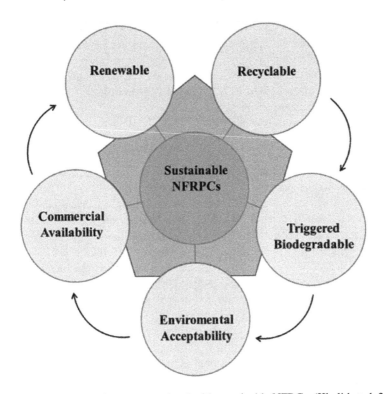

FIGURE 1.10 Common elements correlated with sustainable NFRCs. (Khalid et al. 2021)

in airplane due to the higher strength to weight ratio. Nowadays airplane industry uses 70–80% composite materials in fabricating of structure and it is estimated to contribute 15–20% reduced CO_2 contents till 2050. Further, NFRCs are more environment friendly than traditional composites due to the presence of cellulose, hemicellulose and lignin in fibers. Cellulose is an abundantly available molecule that decomposes naturally. It is understood with the help of one example, i.e. the energy related to burning for China reed strands is assessed to be 14 MJ/kg. Traces of CO_2 emission by this incineration were not found in the atmosphere. Burning natural fiber composites earns positive carbon credits and affects the atmosphere less (Adekomaya et al. 2015; Fernando et al. 2015).

1.12.2 Economic Perspective

Since natural fibers are obtained from living plants and animal skins they are considered ecofriendly materials. It was found in the report of the United States market that the composite market was 2.7 billion pounds in 2006 and that it is expected to grow to 3.3 billion pounds by 2012, with a 3.3% yearly growth rate. Similarly, the average worldwide market for NFRCs was 38% from 2003 to 2007 due to the growing interest in NFRCs after incorporation of environmental regulation

38   Tribology in Sustainable Composites

by governments in industries. Among all markets worldwide, Europe has shown the most significant growth in composite development at 48%, with 0.36 metric tons in 2007 to 3.45 million metric tons in 2020. Therefore, it can be concluded that the industries employing composite materials have proved to be successful businesses all over the world; nowadays NFRCs are effectively contributing to these industries (Adekomaya et al. 2015).

1.13   BIODEGRADABILITY OF SUSTAINABLE COMPOSITES

The NFRCs have shown better biodegradable and renewable properties compared to synthetic fiber composites. The composites converted into CO_2, H_2O, hydrocarbons, methane and biomass using either chemical or biological reaction. Further, the biodegradability test is carried out either by compost test (ASTM D5988/D5338 or ISO 14855) or by soil burial test. The obtained results are presented in the percentage weight loss. But in most of the cases, the soil burial test is applied due to its ease of use. It is found that the different factors such as the molecular weight, chemical structure, glass transition temperature (T_g), melting temperature (T_m), mechanical performance, crystallinity and crystal structure potentially influence the biodegradability of NFRCs (Shih and Huang 2011; Tokiwa and Calabia 2006). It was found that the high temperature and higher crystallinity polymer shows lower weight loss (lower biodegradability) (Tokiwa and Calabia 2006). For example, the biodegradability analysis of the PLA/kenaf fiber composite using garbage processing machine revealed the 38% weight loss within 1 month of composting (Ochi 2008). Several studies show that the biodegradability of composites increases manifold after addition of natural fibers in polymers. Table 1.12 summarizes the biodegradability of different NFRCs from such studies.

1.14   FUTURE TRENDS AND CHALLENGES

In 21st century, natural fiber reinforced composites are undergoing extensive growth with better prospects in constructions and automotive industries for reduction of weight with improved mechanical and thermal properties. It is noticed that bast fibers like kenaf, flax and hemp, etc. are selected for automotive applications. Further, wood plastic composite is the material of choice for construction industries. As per the current trends, Europe and Asia are predicted to be the largest markets for natural fiber reinforced composites because of the environment friendly nature of composite materials. The proper selection of treatment of fibers improves the materials performance. The improved mechanical and thermal properties of fibers create new potential areas in electrical, electronics and sporting equipment. The new potential areas are summarized in Table 1.13.

To achieve long-term durability in outdoors application, these composite materials are needed to overcome weaknesses such as moisture absorption. Extreme weather conditions like temperature, humidity and UV radiation all affect the service life of components using natural fiber reinforced composites.

Sustainable Composites

TABLE 1.12
Biodegradability of the Natural Fiber Reinforced Composites

NFRCs Composition (wt.%)	Biodegradability Test Conditions	Outcomes
Polybutylene succinate (PBS)/ Sugarcane rind fiber (SRF) (95:5)	Soil burial test (100 days)	Maximum weight loss (~20%) was found with the PBS/SRF composites than that of pure PBS (~5%).
Polybutylene adipate-co-terephthalate (PBAT)/ Distillers dried grains with soluble (DDGS) (70:30)	Compost (ASTM D5338)	The PBAT/DDGS composite showed higher biodegradability (~98%) compared to the neat PBAT (~92%).
Polylactic acid (PLA)/Maple wood fiber (70:30)	Compost (ISO-14855)	Acetyl treatment of the maple wood fibers increased their porosity that enhanced the hydrolytic degradation of PLA.
Polypropylene (PP)/Bamboo (50:50)	Soil burial test (ASTM D5988)	15% biodegradability was observed within 130 days.
Polyethylene sebacate (PES)/ Acylated cellulose fiber (85:15)	Compost (ASTM D5338)	Within 30 days, the biocomposite products showed 100% biodegradability.
Polylactic acid (PLA)/Kenaf (80:20) and Polylactic acid (PLA)/Rice husk (80:20)	Soil Burial Test (90 days)	The PLA/Kenaf and PLA/Rice husk composites showed 3-times and 2-times higher weight loss (%), respectively, compared to the neat PLA.
Polylactic acid (PLA)/Soy straw (70:30)	Compost (ASTM D5338)	In 60 days, the PLA/Soy straw exhibited 90% degradation while the pure PLA showed 50%.

Source: Syduzzaman et al. 2020.

1.15 SUMMARY

Because of the government regulation and environment awareness, natural fibers as reinforcement in the fabrication of composite materials for different applications have become popular in the 21st century. The biodegradability and renewable nature of natural fibers make them an ideal replacement for synthetic fibers. There are

40 Tribology in Sustainable Composites

TABLE 1.13
Applications of Natural Fiber Reinforced Composites in Various Fields

Field of Applications	Products
Electrical and Electronics	Antennas, Cable tracks, Windmills, Insulation for electrical construction, Circuit breakers, Printed circuits, Armors, boxes, Television towers – Top
Buildings and Public Works	Facade panels, Covers (domes, windows), Chimneys, Profiles, Partitions, Swimming pool, Concrete molds
Road and Rail Transports	Casings, cabins, Panels, Isothermal trucks, Body components, Power units, wagons, doors, seats, Bottles for gas, Wheels, grills, Ventilation housings, Chassis, Suspension, Highway tankers, Shafts and suspension springs, Trailers
Marine and Cable Transports	Boats: Pleasure and racing canoes, Crafts, Patrol boats, Trawlers, Cabins: Telecabins, Telepherique, Anti-mine ships, Landing gears
Air and Space Transports	Rocket boosters, Shields, Passenger aircrafts and Gliders, Reservoirs, Nozzles, Blades, Propellers, Shafts and Brake discs, Aircraft components: radomes, ailerons, stabilizers
Mechanical applications	Weaving machine rods, Compressed gas bottles, Tubes for offshore platforms, Gears, Bearings, Casings, Pneumatics for radial frames, Jack body, Robot arms, Flywheels, Pipes, Components of drawing table
Sports and Recreation	Skates, Bows and arrows, Rackets, Fishing poles, Javelins, Helmets, Skis, Poles used in jumping, Sails, Surf boards

Source: Ahmed et al. 2018; Puglia et al. 2005; Puttegowda et al. 2018; Sanjay et al. 2016; Sanjay and Siengchin 2018.

two major drawbacks to these fibers extracted from plants and animals: their poor moisture resistance and incompatibility with other fibers limiting their usage in many applications. These can be improved by selecting a proper physical or chemical treatment for these natural fibers. By improving the interface bonding between fibers and matrix, these treatment processes improve the mechanical and thermal properties of composites. Therefore, there is an immense opportunity in the fabrication of new sustainable composites, which reduces further dependence on petroleum reserves.

REFERENCES

Adekomaya O., Jamiru T., Sadiku R. and Huan Z. A review on the sustainability of natural fiber in matrix reinforcement – A practical perspective. *Journal of Reinforced Plastics and Composites,* 35(1), 3–7, 2015.

Adeyi A. J., Durowoju M. O., Adeyi O., Oke E. O., Olalere O. A. and Ogunsola A. D. Momordica augustisepala L. stem fiber reinforced thermoplastic starch: Mechanical property characterization and fuzzy logic artificial intelligent modeling. *Results in Engineering*, 10, 100222, 2021.

Ahmed M. J., Balaji M. S., Saravanakumar S. S., Sanjay M. R. and Senthamaraikannan, P. Characterization of Areva javanica fiber – A possible replacement for synthetic acrylic fiber in the disc brake pad. *Journal of Industrial Textiles*, 49(3), 294–317, 2018.

Al-Maharma, A. and Al-Huniti, N. Critical review of the parameters affecting the effectiveness of moisture absorption treatments used for natural composites. *Journal of Composites Science*, 3(27), 2019.

Alotaibi M. D., Alshammari B. A., Saba N., Alothman O. Y., Sanjay M. R., Almutairi Z. and Jawaid M. Characterization of natural fiber obtained from different parts of date palm tree (Phoenix dactylifera L.). *International Journal of Biological Macromolecules*, 135, 69–76, 2019.

Anbupalani M. S., Venkatachalam C. D. and Rathanasamy R. Influence of coupling agent on altering the reinforcing efficiency of natural fibre-incorporated polymers – A review. *Journal of Reinforced Plastics and Composites*, 39(13–14), 520–544, 2020.

Asumani O. M. L., Reid R. G. and Paskaramoorthy R. The effects of alkali–silane treatment on the tensile and flexural properties of short fibre non-woven kenaf reinforced polypropylene composites. *Composites Part A: Applied Science and Manufacturing*, 43, 1431–1440, 2012.

Atiqah A., Jawaid M., Ishak M. R. and Sapuan S. M. Effect of alkali and silane treatments on mechanical and interfacial bonding strength of sugar palm fibers with thermoplastic polyurethane. *Journal of Natural Fibers*, 15, 251–261, 2018.

Bhat K. M., Rajagopalan J., Mallikarjunaiah R., Rao N. N. and Sharma A. Eco-friendly and biodegradable green composites, in *Biocomposites [Working Title]*, ed. Brajesh Kumar (London: IntechOpen), 2021. https://doi.org/10.5772/intechopen.98687

Bunsell A. R. (ed.). Introduction to the science of fibers, in *Handbook of Properties of Textile and Technical Fibres* (Woodhead Publishing), 1–20, 2018.

Chaudhary V., Bajpai P. K. and Maheswari S. An investigation on wear and dynamic mechanical behavior of jute/hemp/flax reinforced composites and its hybrids for tribological applications. *Fibers and Polymers*, 19(2), 403–415, 2018.

Colomban P. and Jauzein V. Silk: Fibers, films, and composites-types, processing, structure, and mechanics, in *Handbook of Properties of Textile and Technical Fibres*, ed. A. R. Bunsell (Woodhead Publishing), 137–183, 2018.

Cummings A. J. and Olse M. Mechanism of action of stinging nettles. *Wilderness & Environmental Medicine*, 22, 136–139, 2011.

Das S. and Natarajan G. Silk fiber composites in biomedical applications, in *Materials for Biomedical Engineering*, eds. V. Grumezescu and A. Mihai Grumezescu (Elsevier), 309–338, 2019.

Debeli D. K., Qin Z. and Guo J. Study on the pre-treatment, physical and chemical properties of ramie fibers reinforced poly (Lactic Acid) (PLA) biocomposite. *Journal of Natural Fibers*, 15, 596–610, 2018.

Fernando A. L., Duarte M. P., Vatsanidou A. and Alexopoulou E. Environmental aspects of fiber crops cultivation and use, *Industrial Crops and Products*, 68, 105–115, 2015.

Jawaid M. and Abdul Khalil H. P. S. Cellulosic/synthetic fiber reinforced polymer hybrid composites: A review. *Carbohydrate Polymers*, 86(1), 1–18, 2011.

Jena H. and Katiyar J. K. Study of tribo-corrosion in materials, in *Advances in Engine Tribology. Energy, Environment, and Sustainability*, eds. V. Kumar, A. K. Agarwal, A. Jena and R. K. Upadhyay (Singapore: Springer), 239–256, 2022.

Joshi S. V., Drzal L. T., Mohanty A. K. and Arora S. Are natural fiber composites environmentally superior to glass fiber reinforced composites? *Composites Part A: Applied Science and Manufacturing*, 35(3), 371–376, 2004.

Katiyar J. K., Hammad J. A. and Samad M. A. Tribological properties of light metal matrix composites, in *Encyclopedia of Materials: Composites,* ed. D. Brabazon (Elsevier), 1, 389–401, 2021.

Katiyar J. K. and Sahu R. K. *Modern Manufacturing Technology: Spotlight on Future* (1st ed.). CRC Press, 2021. https://doi.org/10.1201/9781003203162

Khalid M. Y., Rashid A. A., Arif Z. U., Ahmed W., Arshad H. and Zadi A. A. Natural fiber reinforced composites: Sustainable materials for emerging applications. *Result in Engineering,* 11, 100263, 2021.

Khan M. A., Hassan M. M., Taslima R. and Mustafa A. I. Role of pretreatment with potassium permanganate and urea on mechanical and degradable properties of photocured coir (cocos nucifera) fiber with 1,6-hexanediol diacrylate. *Journal of Applied Polymer Science,* 100, 4361–4368, 2006.

Kipriotis E., Heping X., Vafeiadakis T., Kiprioti M. and Alexopoulou, E. Ramie and kenaf as feed crops. *Industrial Crops and Products,* 68, 126–130, 2015.

Lee B. H., Kim H. J. and Yu W. R. Fabrication of long and discontinuous natural fiber reinforced polypropylene biocomposites and their mechanical properties. *Fiber and Polymers,* 10, 83–90, 2009.

Li, X., Tabil, L. G. and Panigrahi, S. Chemical treatments of natural fiber for use in natural fiber-reinforced composites: A review. *Journal of Polymers and the Environment,* 15, 25–33, 2007.

Martins A. B. and Santana R. M. C. Effect of carboxylic acids as compatibilizer agent on mechanical properties of thermoplastic starch and polypropylene blends. *Carbohydrate Polymers,* 135, 79–85, 2016.

MR S., Siengchin S., Parameswaranpillai J., Jawaid M., Pruncu C. I. and Khan A. A comprehensive review of techniques for natural fibers as reinforcement in composites: Preparation, processing and characterization. *Carbohydrate Polymers,* 207, 108–121, 2019.

Nassar M. M. A., Alzebdeh K. I., Pervez T. and Munam A. Progress and challenges in sustainability, compatibility, and production of eco-composites: A state-of-art review. *Journal of Applied Polymer Science,* 138(43), 51284, 2021.

Nurazzi N. M., Harussani M. M., Aisyah H. A., Ilyas R. A., Norrrahim M. N. F., Khalina A. and Abdullah, N. Treatments of natural fiber as reinforcement in polymer composites-a short review. *Functional Composites and Structures,* 3(2), 024002, 2021.

Ochi S. Mechanical properties of kenaf fibers and kenaf/PLA composites. *Mechanics of Materials,* 40, 446–452, 2008.

Omar M. F., Jaya H. and Zulkepli, N. N. Kenaf fiber reinforced composite in the automotive industry. *Encyclopedia of Renewable and Sustainable Materials,* 5, 95–101, 2019.

Paul A., Joseph K. and Thomas S. Effect of surface treatments on the electrical properties of low-density polyethylene composites reinforced with short sisal fibers. *Composites Science and Technology,* 57, 67–79, 1997.

Peças P., Carvalho H., Salman H. and Leite M. Natural fibre composites and their applications: A review. *Journal of Composite Science,* 2(4), 66, 2018.

Pham L. J. *Coconut (Cocos nucifera)* (AOCS Press), 2016.

Prachayawarakorn J., Chaiwatyothin S., Mueangta S. and Hanchana A. Effect of jute and kapok fibers on properties of thermoplastic cassava starch composites. *Materials Design,* 47, 309–315, 2013.

Puglia D., Biagiotti J. and Kenny J. M., A review on natural fiber-based composites – Part II: Application of natural reinforcements in composite materials for automotive industry. *Journal of Natural Fibers,* 1(3), 23–65, 2005.

Sustainable Composites

Puttegowda M., Rangappa S. M., Jawaid M., Shivanna P., Basavegowda Y., Saba N., Potential of natural/synthetic hybrid composites for aerospace applications, in *Woodhead Publishing Series in Composites Science and Engineering, Sustainable Composites for Aerospace Applications*, eds. M. Jawaid, M. Thariq, (Woodhead Publishing), 315–351, 2018.

Rajak D. K., Pagar D. D., Menezes P. L. and Linul E. Fiber-reinforced polymer composites: Manufacturing, properties, and applications. *Polymers,* 11, 1667, 2019.

Ramesh, M. Flax (Linum usitatissimum L.) fibre reinforced polymer composite materials: A review on preparation, properties and prospects. *Progress in Materials Science,* 102, 109–166, 2019.

Réquilé S., Le Duigou A., Bourmaud A. and Baley C. Peeling experiments for hemp retting characterization targeting biocomposites. *Industrial Crops and Products,* 123, 573–580, 2018.

Rong M. Z., Zhang M. Q., Liu Y., Yang G. C. and Zeng H. M. The effect of fiber treatment on the mechanical properties of unidirectional sisal-reinforced epoxy composites. *Composites Science and Technology,* 61, 1437–1447, 2001.

Sanjay M. R., Arpitha G. R., Naik L. L., Gopalakrishna K. and Yogesha B. Applications of natural fibers and its composites: An overview. *Natural Resources,* 7(3), 108–114, 2016.

Sanjay M. R. and Siengchin S. Natural fibers as perspective materials. *KMUTNB International Journal of Applied Science and Technology,* 11, 233, 2018.

Saravanakumaar A., Senthilkumar A., Saravanakumar S. S. and Sanjay M. R. Impact of alkali treatment on physico-chemical, thermal, structural and tensile properties of Carica papaya bark fibers. *International Journal of Polymer Analysis and Characterization,* 23, 529–536, 2018.

Shahinur S. and Hasan M. Jute/coir/banana fiber reinforced biocomposites: Critical review of design, fabrication, properties and applications, in *Reference Module in Materials Science and Materials Engineering,* ed. S. Hashmi and I. A. Choudhury (Elsevier Ltd.), 751–756, 2019.

Shesan O. J., Stephen A. C., Chioma A. G., Neerish R. and Rotimi S. E. Improving the mechanical properties of natural fiber composites for structural and biomedical applications, in *Renewable and Sustainable Composites.* eds. A. B. Pereira and F. A. O. Fernandes. Intechopen UK, 2019. https://doi.org/10.5772/intechopen.85252

Shih Y. F. and Huang C. C. Polylacticacid (PLA)/bananafibre (BF) biodegradable greencomposites. *Journal of Polymer Research,* 18, 2335–2340, 2011.

Sreekala M. S. and Thomas S. Effect of fibre surface modification on water-sorption characteristics of oil palm fibres. *Composites Science and Technology,* 63, 861–869, 2003.

Syduzzaman Md., Al Faruque A. Md., Bilisik K. and Naebe M. Plant-based natural fibre reinforced composites: A review on fabrication. *Properties and Applications, Coatings,* 10, 973, 2020.

Thyavihalli Girijappa Y. G., Mavinkere Rangappa S., Parameswaranpillai J. and Siengchin S. Natural fibers as sustainable and renewable resource for development of eco-friendly composites: A comprehensive review. *Frontiers in Materials,* 6, 226, 2019.

Tokiwa Y. and Calabia B. P. Biodegradability and biodegradation of poly (lactide). *Applied Microbiology and Biotechnology,* 72, 244–251, 2006.

Wang G. and Chen F. Development of bamboo fiber-based composites, in *Advanced High Strength Natural Fiber Composites in Construction,* eds. M. Fan and F. Fu (Elsevier Ltd.), 235–255, 2016.

Willberg-Keyriläinen P., Hiltunen J. and Ropponen J. Production of cellulose carbamate using urea-based deep eutectic solvents. *Cellulose,* 25, 195–204, 2018.

Zafeiropoulos N. E. and Baillie C. A. A study of the effect of surface treatments on the tensile strength of flax fibres: Part II. Application of Weibull statistics. *Composites Part A: Applied Science Manufacturing* 38, 629–638, 2007.

Zaman H. U., Khan M. A., Khan R. A., Rahman M. A., Das L. R. and Al-Mamun, M. Role of potassium permanganate and urea on the improvement of the mechanical properties of jute polypropylene composites. *Fibers and Polymers,* 11, 455–463, 2010.

Zhang M. Q., Rong M. Z. and Lu X. (2005). Fully biodegradable natural fiber composites from renewable resources: All-plant fiber composites. *Composites Science and Technology,* 65, 2514–2525, 2005.

2 Factors Affecting the Properties of Sustainable Composites

2.1 INTRODUCTION

During the past few decades, natural fibers have gradually replaced synthetic fiber composites due to the non-biodegradability, toxicity, non-recyclability, etc. of synthetic fibers. Natural fibers are now widely used as reinforcement in a composite as they are biodegradable, recyclable and easily available in huge quantities. These reinforced composites can be used in automotive and aerospace as they make a vehicle lightweight and thereby help improve fuel efficiency and save energy. These composites are also known as biocomposites or sustainable composites. They are made up of natural fibers in either biodegradable or non-biodegradable matrices (Lu et al. 2013). As a result of their higher strength, greater rigidity and combined low weight, Fiber Reinforced Polymer (FRP) is used to fabricate a wide range of structures. The thermoset and thermoplastic polymer resin and synthetic fibers such as basalt fibers and carbon fibers are commonly used as matrix with FRP as reinforcement. Further, the Natural Fiber Reinforced Polymer Composites (NFRPCs) have several advantages, including low weight, biodegradability, low cost and great mechanical qualities. The use of NFRPCs in engineering applications is justified because their mechanical strength is equivalent to that of synthetic fibers, and their lower environmental impact contributes to a cleaner environment. However, regulating and increasing the mechanical properties of NFRPCs is quite difficult. Because of its widespread availability, low cost and thermoplastic nature, starch is the most promising polymer for making films. Nevertheless, this polymer has severe shortcomings in terms of its hydrophilic property, difficulty in handling and poor mechanical behavior. Therefore, it is important to understand the factors that affect the properties of NFRPs. Figure 2.1 shows the factors contributing to the performance of biocomposites originating from natural fibers. Even though the factors are briefly defined in Chapter 1, a few important factors such as fiber orientation, fiber dispersion, fiber length and fiber concentration are described in following subsections.

2.2 FIBER CONCENTRATION

The concentration of fibers is very important in the development of composites. Fibers are added in matrix either by weight percentage or volume percentage. To achieve

DOI: 10.1201/9781003270966-2

45

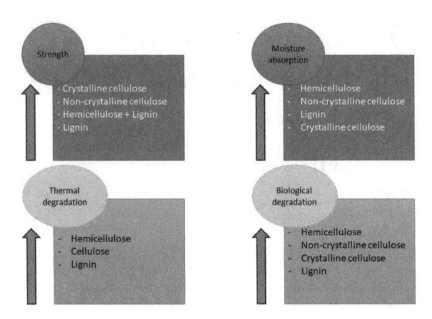

FIGURE 2.1 Factors contributing to the diverse properties of natural fibers. (Nurazzi et al. 2021)

desirable properties, it is important to optimize the fiber concentration in matrix. The higher concentration of fibers in matrix results in the agglomeration of fibers, causing poor dispersion and formation of excessive cavities. Therefore, the biocomposites can be produced with fiber volume fractions ranging from 20 to 40% by weight (Lu et al. 2013). Further, fiber concentration is one of the important factors affecting the tensile strength of the composite. Udaya Kiran et al. (2007) experimentally investigated biocomposites with different concentrations and different fiber lengths. They found that both fiber length and concentration are equally important to achieve higher tensile strength. Moreover, the banana fiber reinforced polyester matrix showed a tensile strength of about 59 MPa with a fiber length of 3 cm and 51 wt.%. Similarly, the hemp fiber exhibited a tensile strength of 59.53 MPa with a fiber length of 3 cm and 56 wt.%. Furthermore, fique fiber polyester composites were studied for ballistics testing with various volume fractions of fique fibers such as 10%, 20% and 30%. The findings showed that the biocomposites with 30% fiber volume fractions are suitable candidates for multilayered armor systems and can even replace Kevlar because of their high energy absorption capacity and high impact integrity (Pereira et al. 2019).

Garcia Filho et al. (2020) has also investigated experimentally the use of piassava fiber as reinforcement in epoxy resin type bisphenol-A diglycidyl ether (DGEBA) hardened with triethylenetetramine (TETA) with different weight percentages as shown in Table 2.1. For comparing the results with the commercial Kevlar material, the composites were ballistically evaluated against the 7.62 mm high impact energy ammunition in a standalone test. The test revealed that the 10 wt.% concentration

Factors Affecting the Properties of Sustainable Composites

TABLE 2.1
Limit Velocity for Biocomposites

S.no	Condition	Velocity Limits
1	PRE10	236 ± 8
2	PRE20	200 ± 9
3	PRE30	202 ± 7
4	PRE40	198 ± 6
5	PRE50	204 ± 2
6	Epoxy/Mallow fibers	231 ± 18
7	Polyester/Curaua fibers	207 ± 21
8	Kevlar™	212 ± 23

Source: Garcia Filho et al. 2020.

of natural fiber showed best results compared to the commercial Kevlar material. Further, increasing the weight percentage of the natural fiber decreases the velocity limit of the composite. Therefore, the concentration of the fiber depends on the types of fibers used for a particular application. Moreover, Nassar et al. (2021) found that there is a strong relationship between length of a fiber and its orientation, with mechanical properties such as tensile strength. They noticed that the lengthy fibers have a higher tensile strength. Adding up to 40 wt.% cocoa waste to recycled low density polyethylene (rLDPE) reduces strength and elongation and increases material stiffness. Fiber malleting with rLDPE caused poor homogeneity and compatibility between corn husk fibers and rLDPE when fiber loading exceeded 20 wt.%.

Furthermore, Mohammed et al. (2016) performed surface treatment of sugar palm fiber with various concentrations of NaOH (2%, 4% and 6%). The 30 wt.% sugar palm fiber with fixed fiber size at 250 μm was blended with thermoplastic polyurethane composites. At 2% NaOH concentration, the treated fiber has a tensile modulus of 440 MPa and a tensile strain of 41.6% at 6% NaOH concentration. Despite this, the tensile strength of composite fibers was lower than that of the untreated fibers. It was concluded that NaOH deposits on the sugar palm fiber surface reduced the tensile strength after the chemical treatment. Although chemical treatment can improve the mechanical properties of natural fibers, other fibers may have to undergo physical treatment or functionalization process as they may get affected.

Thomason et al. (1997) conducted an experiment on the effect of fiber length and its concentration in polypropylene composite for investigating their mechanical properties such as tensile strength, flexural strength, modulus and impact strength (shown in Table 2.2). As observed from Table 2.2, the Charpy impact strength increases with increases in fiber concentration; the Charpy impact strength increases initially with fiber length but levels out above 6 mm. The Charpy impact strength is relatively insensitive to test temperature between –50°C and 40°C, which shows

TABLE 2.2
Influence of Fiber Length and Concentration on the Mechanical Properties of Polypropylene

	Conc. % Weight	Fiber Length (mm)					
		0.09	0.8	3	4.5	6	12
Tensile modulus (GPa)	10			2.45	2.47	2.5	2.54
	25	2.86		4.11	4.26	4.47	4.63
	30		4.79	4.86	5.03	5.23	4.94
Flexural modulus (GPa)	10			2.53	2.45	2.49	2.46
	20			3.51	3.54	3.62	3.23
	25	2.79		4	4.03	3.94	3.98
	30		4.49	5.04	4.75	4.75	4.71
	40			5.86	5.91	5.4	5.95
Tensile Strength (Mpa)	10			36.1	39	36.5	40.9
	25	27.2		49.6	55.9	56.9	57.8
	30		50.7	56.8	62.3	61.6	69.2
Flexural strength (MPa)	10			64.1	65.7	67.2	72.2
	20			80	82.2	91.6	85.4
	25	47.2		86.7	91.4	93.7	103.5
	30		75	123.2	124.5	119.7	130.9
Charpy impact, 23°C (kJ m^{-2})	10			7.9	8.6	8.2	9.6
	20			12.6	14.2	16	19.4
	25	1.9		14.3	17.6	20.1	24.5
	30		7.6	19	21.3	23.3	27.6
	40			28	31.2	37.6	41.2

Source: Thomason et al. 1997.

only a slight increase with decreasing temperature. Further, the use of a glass fiber with improved polypropylene sizing compatibility has doubled the Charpy impact strength. The stiffest, strongest and most impact-resistant polypropylene is made of PPG 803 1 glass fibers, with a fiber length of > 8 mm. Moreover, similar trend has been noticed for other mechanical properties that increase with fiber length.

2.3 FIBER ORIENTATION

Nature employs the principle of optimized reinforcing fiber orientation to create plant structures that can withstand natural stresses such as wind force. Further, the fiber-reinforced polymers have a number of advantages over other polymer composites, including low weight, corrosion resistance, high tensile strength and high elastic modulus. But, the issue of moisture absorption occurs when biocomposites are

Factors Affecting the Properties of Sustainable Composites

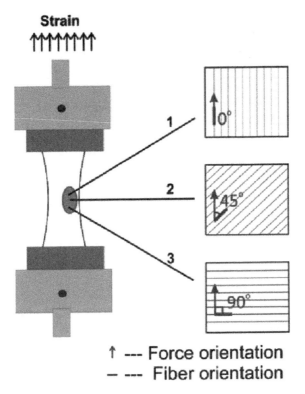

FIGURE 2.2 Schematic representation of stretching composite for several orientations of the fibers. (Maciel et al. 2018)

exposed to humid air or are submerged in water. The absorbed water collects at the fiber-matrix interface, causing debonding. It was reported that the composites absorb water which is about 30% of their weight, making a significant impact on the elastic-modulus and other performance characteristics. Figure 2.2 shows the schematic representation of different mechanical experiments, where stretching was applied along different angles with respect to the orientation of the fibers. It was observed that the properties improved more at 0° orientation as compared to 45° and 90° orientation of fibers. This is mainly due to the presence of less fiber in the stretching direction at 45° and 90° orientation than 0° orientation of the fibers.

Furthermore, cellulose type lyocell fibers (CLY) are used in polypropylene at different fiber orientations and their effect on elastic modulus is analyzed. The orientations of 0°, ± 22.5°, ± 45°, ± 67.5° and 90° are used in 62% w/w PP and 38% w/w lyocell fibers. Figure 2.3 shows that the zero degree fiber orientation has a better elastic modulus than any other orientation of fiber arrangement. This is due to the presence of more fiber at 0° orientation. Moreover, when subjected to the same direction of fiber orientation as stretching, the strain value at break is increased; however, when the angle between stretching direction and fiber orientation is 90°,

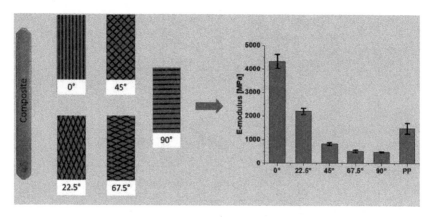

FIGURE 2.3 Effect of reinforcement fiber orientation on mechanical properties of lyocell-reinforced polypropylene composite. (Cordin et al. 2018)

TABLE 2.3
Properties of Fiber Based on Angle

Fibers	Cellulose (Wt.%)	Density (g/cm3)	Moisture Content (Wt.%)	Microfibrillar Angle (degrees)	Young's Modulus (Gpa)	Tensile Strength (Mpa)	Elongation
Coir	31–42	1.1	10	30–40	4–6	106–175	17–47
Banana	17	1.3	7	10	7–20	54–754	10.35
Sisal	64–70	1.45	10	10–22	9–15	568–640	3–7
Pineapple Leaf	20–80	1.44	12	8–14	34–82	413–1627	0.8–1

Source: Khalid et al. 2021.

the strain value at break decreases. This is due to the presence of fewer fibers at the stretching direction.

Further, Table 2.3 shows the properties of the natural fiber and the . Suarez et al. (1986) demonstrated analytical predictions as well as the experimentation of the damping on the basis of their aspect ratio. The theoretical analysis shows the best damping but when it was experimented, the damping was found to be lower than the analytical data. However, the projected tendency of greater damping when the aspect ratio is lowered was confirmed by experimental results.

Furthermore, when the fiber angle is away from the zero, the off-axis composite properties are virtually independent of the fiber aspect ratio in the range of practical aspect ratios. In graphite/epoxy and aramid/epoxy, higher experimental damping values were obtained by altering the fiber orientation than by varying the fiber aspect

Factors Affecting the Properties of Sustainable Composites   51

ratio. Therefore, it is necessary to control the lamina orientation in a continuous fiber-reinforced laminate, rather than controlling the fiber aspect ratio. It may be a superior way to increase composite damping.

2.4 FIBER DISPERSION

The dispersion of the fiber material to the matrix is very much important for obtaining good mechanical properties. The interaction between natural fibers and polymer matrix is quite weak due to the hydrophilic nature of the fibers. A minor change in parameters during the processing of composite, such as mixing speed, pressure and temperature, will affect the properties of the final product. Polymer blends are described as a mixture of two or more polymers designed to improve the qualities of products while lowering the cost. Polymer blends can simply be considered as polymer alloys. Nassar et al. (2021) found the irregular geometry of natural fibers that are responsible for lowering the strength of ecocomposites due to weak interfacial regions, poor compatibility and wetting between polar plant fibers and non-polar polymers. The interfacial adhesion between fiber and matrix can be improved either by physical treatment or by chemical treatment or functionalization of fibers and polymers. Each of the three techniques has been described in detail in Chapter 1 and is briefly described in the following section.

2.5 FIBER TREATMENT

Plant fibers are treated in order to improve their cellulose content, their interfacial adhesion to polymer matrix and their mechanical, thermal and dimensional stability properties. The surface modification can take the form of physical, chemical or biological processes. The use of plasma and corona treatment, to modify the fiber surface, is one of the physical methods of surface modification. This aids in the creation of rough surfaces due to which mechanical interlocking is improved. On the other hand, plasma treatment can be used to impart chemical functionality on fibers, allowing them to react chemically with the polymer matrix. Liu et al. (2004) dispersed the grass fiber in matrix and investigated their properties with respect to treatment time and concentration of alkali solution. When compared to raw fiber reinforced soy-based biocomposites, the impact strength of alkali-treated grass fiber reinforced soy-based biocomposites was increased by nearly 40%. With increasing alkali solution concentration and treatment duration, the tensile and flexural characteristics of alkali-treated grass fiber reinforced soy-based biocomposites improved steadily. This is due to the fact that alkali treatment promoted fiber dispersion in the matrix, which boosted fiber reinforcement efficiency in the matrix. Additionally, after alkali treatment, the grass fiber surface contained more hydroxyl groups, resulting in greater fiber-matrix interfacial adhesion. Further, the proper treatment of natural fibers confirms the removal of low molar mass impurities including wax and oil, which make the fiber surface rougher, resulting in better interfacial bonding between fibers and the surrounding matrix (Shalwan et al. 2013).

2.6 EFFECT OF NANO MATERIAL IN NATURAL FIBER COMPOSITE

It is well known that nanomaterial is the future material for improving the mechanical properties of composites. Nassar et al. (2020), in an experiment, analyzed the influence of fiberglass and a small amount of Nano filler in the resin on the mechanical properties and thermal properties of multilayered laminate composites. They found that the continuous fiber glass has shown 17% to 24% better impact strength compared to the random fiberglass. Further, the dispersion of 0.5 wt.% of Graphene Nanoplatelets (GnP) resulted in maximum tensile strength of 312 MPa in the continuous fiberglass. Moreover, the impact of strength improved from 0 to 0.4 wt.% for both types of fiberglass, and then drops for 0.5 wt.% GnP filler content. Similarly, Devnani et al. (2019) stated that the addition of very less amount of nanofiller does not affect the density of the product but improves the mechanical and thermal properties of composites. Therefore, researchers have tried to incorporate nano clay, SiO_2, carbon nanotubes and many other nanofillers to improve the characteristics of natural fiber reinforced polymer composites. Among all, nano clay has demonstrated its ability to reduce the water absorption in sisal fiber reinforced composites, which is extremely desirable, and SiO_2 has proven to be very effective in improving the mechanical properties of these composites. Furthermore, carbon nanotubes have been shown to be useful in improving the mechanical and water absorption properties of bamboo and ramie fiber reinforced polymer composites. Table 2.4 summarizes the data pertaining to the effect of nanofillers on the properties of NFRCs.

2.7 LIFE-CYCLE ASSESSMENT OF NATURAL FIBER REINFORCED COMPOSITES (NFRCs)

The life cycle assessment (LCA) of NFRCs composites (shown in Figure 2.4) is a part of ISO14000 series of the Environmental Management System. It estimates the overall impact of NFRCs on the environment throughout the whole life cycle starting from extraction of fibers to its disposal.

Further, different studies have been carried out to analyze the LCA of NFRCs that is presented in Table 2.5. These studies reveal that the NFRCs have shown significant superior environmental performance compared to synthetic fiber reinforced composites.

2.8 SUMMARY

It was observed that fiber orientation, fiber length, fiber dispersion, fiber types and polymer type play a very important role in the performance of NFRCs. Further, to improve the properties of NFRCs, the treatment of fibers are important. It can be carried out either physically or chemically. Moreover, the hybridization with synthetic fiber laminates on Natural filler composite can improve moisture absorption capabilities as well as nobler mechanical properties. Synthetic fibers such as glass fiber or carbon filaments are immune to moisture absorption and have a higher mechanical strength than natural fibers.

TABLE 2.4

Effect of Nano Fillers on the Properties of Natural Fiber Reinforced Composites

Matrix	Reinforcement Fiber	Nano Filler Used	Application of That Nano Filler	Loading Percentage of Fiber and Clay	Method	Improvement in Mechanical and Water Absorption Properties Property as Compared to Absence of Nanofiller
Poly propylene	Wood flour	Mont morillonite (MMT)-based nanoclay Cloisite 20A	Material applications	30% fiber loading and clay loading is from 0 to 6% and coupling agent maleated polypropyl ene from 0 to 7.5%	Injection molding	(a) Improvement in tensile strength by 20% and flexural strength by 13% (b) Composites prepared with 3% nanoclay exhibited lower water absorption
Epoxy	Sisal	Mont morillonite (MMT)-based nanoclay Cloisite 30B	Drug delivery carriers, Material applications Rheology, modifiers, Gas absorbents, Nano composites	50% fiber loading and clay loading is from 2 to 5%	Vacuum assisted resin infusion molding	(a) 27% increase in tensile strength and 47% increase in tensile modulus (b) Uptake in equilibrium water is reduced to one third in case of 5% nanoclay filled composites

(*continued*)

TABLE 2.4 (Continued)
Effect of Nano Fillers on the Properties of Natural Fiber Reinforced Composites

Matrix	Reinforcement Fiber	Nano Filler Used	Application of That Nano Filler	Loading Percentage of Fiber and Clay	Method	Improvement in Mechanical and Water Absorption Properties Property as Compared to Absence of Nanofiller
Unsaturated polyester resin partially substituted by epoxi dized soybean oil	Hemp	Cloisite 30B		21–22% fiber loading and clay loading is 0 to 1.5%	Compression molding	(a) Decrease in ultimate tensile strength by 20% (b) Moisture absorption reduced by 8%
High density Poly ethylene	Bamboo	Montmorillonite clay filler		25 to 30% fiber loading and clay loading is from 0 to 5%	Melt compounding	Addition of clay led to negative effect on mechanical properties
Poly propylene	Sisal	Organically modified mont morillonite (MMT)-based nanoclay Cloisite 30B		10–40% fiber loading and with 5 gm of maleic anhydride grafted poly propylene	Compression molding	(a) Composites with 5% coupling agent, 5% nanoclay, 40% treated fibers showed best tensile strength (b) Composites with 5% nanoclay have less water absorption but not less as compared to coupling agent alone

Polyester	Sisal	Nanoclay (Garamite)	Rheology modifier	25% fiber loading and 3% clay	Compression molding	(a) Substantial increase in mechanical properties (b) Decrease in water absorption
High density poly ethylene	Bagasse fiber	Nano -SiO_2	Improves concrete workability, bio medical applications	40% fiber loading and 2 and 5% Nano -SiO_2	Injection molding	(a) 5% nanoSiO_2 added samples show 71.46% increase in tensile strength (b) No significant change in water absorption
Urea Formal dehyde	Wood	Nano -SiO_2	Improves concrete workability, bio medical applications	20% wood and 1% nano SiO_2	Pressurized impre gnation	(a) Most of the properties have been improved (b) Decreased water absorption
Ethylene covinyl acetate	Sugar cane Bagasse	TiO_2	Used in polymers as white pigment,	0 to 30% fiber loading and 0 to 2% TiO_2 loading	Melt mixed intercalation method	10% increase in tensile strength after addition of TiO_2
Epoxy	Bamboo	Carbon nano tubes (CNT)	Energy storage, Air and water filtration, Biomedical applications	-	Hand lay up	(a) 6.67% increase in tensile strength and 5.8% in flexural strength (b) Water absorption is reduced from 26.28% to 23.18%
Epoxy	Ramie	Carbon nano tubes (CNT)	Molecular electronics, Fibers and fabrics	Carbon nano tube addition from 0 to 0.6%	Hand lay up	Flexural strength and flexural modulus improved by 34% and 37%

(continued)

TABLE 2.4 (Continued)
Effect of Nano Fillers on the Properties of Natural Fiber Reinforced Composites

Matrix	Reinforcement Fiber	Nano Filler Used	Application of That Nano Filler	Loading Percentage of Fiber and Clay	Method	Improvement in Mechanical and Water Absorption Properties Property as Compared to Absence of Nanofiller
Poly propylene	Bagasse	Nano-graphene	Bio medical applications, semi-conductors	Fiber loading 15 and 30% Nano graphene 0.1 to 1%	Melt compounding	(a) Composites containing 0.1% NG and 30% bagasse fiber show highest tensile, flexural and impact properties (b) No significant change in water absorption
Epoxy	Jute	Graphene	Electronic devices	25% fiber and 0.3,1,3% graphene	Hand lay up	Graphene as nanofiller enhanced the machinability of composite material
Epoxy	Kenaf	Mont morillonite	Material applications	3% nano filler	Hand lay up	Oil palm nano filler addition marked a 24.9% increase in tensile strength and 28.3% increase in impact strength

Source: Devnania and Sinha 2019.

Factors Affecting the Properties of Sustainable Composites

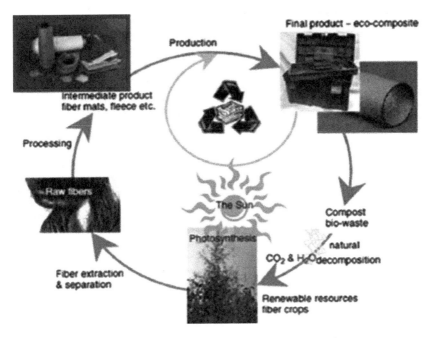

FIGURE 2.4 Demonstration of life cycle of NFRCs. (Faruk et al. 2014)

TABLE 2.5
Summarized Data on Life Cycle Assessment of NFRCs

Composite	Application	Life-Cycle Approach	Remarks
Hemp fiber/epoxy versus ABS	Side-panel component for passenger car (Audi A3)	Cradle-to-grave	Cumulative energy demand of hemp fiber/ epoxy composite was 45% lower than that of ABS
Hemp fiber/ Triglycerides and polycarbon acid anhydrides (PTP) versus hemp fiber/ polyester	Bus body component	Cradle-to-grave	Composite with PTP had 65% and 39% lower energy demand and global warming potential than those with polyester, respectively
Curaua fiber/ polypropylene versus glass fiber/ polypropylene	Automotive internal component	Cradle-to-grave	Curaua fiber/polypropylene composite had 75% and 66% lower climate change and ozone depletion potential than those of glass fiber/ polypropylene, respectively

(*continued*)

TABLE 2.5 (Continued)
Summarized Data on Life Cycle Assessment of NFRCs

Composite	Application	Life-Cycle Approach	Remarks
Hemp fiber/PTP versus glass fiber/polyester	Bus body component	Cradle-to-grave	Hemp fiber/PTP composite had 54% and 44% lower global warming and climate change potential than those of glass fiber/polyester, respectively
Sugarcane bagasse fiber/polypropylene versus talc/polypropylene	Vehicle interior aesthetic covering component	Cradle-to-grave	Sugarcane bagasse fiber/polypropylene had 20% and 25% lower energy demand and global warming impact than those of talc/polypropylene, respectively
Kenaf fiber/soy-based resin versus glass fiber/polyester	Sheet molding compound material	Cradle-to-grate	Kenaf fiber/soy-based resin composite had 58%, 13%, 97% and 22% lower global warming, ozone depletion, hedgehog cancer and ecotoxicity potential than those of glass fiber/polyester composite, respectively
Hybrid glass-hemp fiber/epoxy versus glass fiber/epoxy	Elbow fittings for the seawater cooling pipeline	Cradle-to-grave	Hybrid glass-hemp fiber/epoxy composite had 18%, 19%, 20% and 20% lower global energy requirement, global warming potential, ecotoxicity and life cycle cost than those of glass fiber/epoxy composite, respectively

Source: Gholampour and Ozbakkaloglu 2020.

REFERENCES

Cordin M., Bechtold T. and Pham T. Effect of fibre orientation on the mechanical properties of polypropylene–lyocell composites. *Cellulose,* 25, 7197–7210, 2018.

Devnani G. L. and Sinha S. Effect of nanofillers on the properties of natural fiber reinforced polymer composites. *Materials Today: Proceedings,* 18, 647–654. 2019. https://doi.org/10.1016/j.matpr.2019.06.460

Faruk O., Bledzki A. K., Fink H. P. and Sain M. Progress report on natural fiber reinforced composites. *Macromolecular Materials & Engineering*, 299(1), 9–26, 2014.

Garcia Filho F. D. C., Oliveira M. S., Pereira A. C., Nascimento L. F. C., Ricardo Gomes Matheus J. and Monteiro S. N. Ballistic behavior of epoxy matrix composites reinforced with piassava fiber against high energy ammunition. *Journal of Materials Research and Technology*, 9(2), 1734–1741. 2020. https://doi.org/10.1016/j.jmrt.2019.12.004

Gholampour A. and Ozbakkaloglu T. A review of natural fiber composites: Properties, modification and processing techniques, characterization, applications, *Journal of Materials Science,* 55, 829–892, 2020.

Khalid M. Y., Al Rashid A., Arif Z. U., Ahmed W., Arshad H. and Zaidi A. A. Natural fiber reinforced composites: Sustainable materials for emerging applications. *Results in Engineering*, 11(April), 100263, 2021. https://doi.org/10.1016/j.rineng.2021.100263

Liu W., Mohanty A. K., Askeland P., Drzal L. T. and Misra M. Influence of fiber surface treatment on properties of Indian grass fiber reinforced soy protein based biocomposites. *Polymer*, 45(22), 7589–7596, 2004. https://doi.org/10.1016/j.polymer.2004.09.009

Lu N. and Oza S. Thermal stability and thermo-mechanical properties of hemp-high density polyethylene composites: Effect of two different chemical modifications. *Composites Part B: Engineering*, 44(1), 484–490, 2013. https://doi.org/10.1016/j.composit esb.2012.03.024

Maciel M. M., Ribeiro S., Ribeiro C., Francesko A., Maceiras A., Vilas J. L. and Lanceros-Méndez S. Relation between fiber orientation and mechanical properties of nano-engineered poly(vinylidene fluoride) electrospun composite fiber mats, *Composites Part B: Engineering*, 139, 146–154, 2018.

Mohammed A. A., Bachtiar D., Siregar J. P. and Rejab M. R. M. Effect of sodium hydroxide on the tensile properties of sugar palm fibre reinforced thermoplastic polyurethane composites. *Journal of Mechanical Engineering and Sciences*, 10(1), 1765–1777, 2016. https://doi.org/10.15282/jmes.10.1.2016.2.0170

Nassar A. and Nassar E. Effect of fiber orientation on the mechanical properties of multi layers laminate nanocomposites. *Heliyon*, 6(1), e03167, 2020. https://doi.org/10.1016/j.heli yon.2020.e03167

Nassar M. M. A., Alzebdeh K. I., Pervez T., Al-Hinai N. and Munam A. Progress and challenges in sustainability, compatibility, and production of eco-composites: A state-of-art review. *Journal of Applied Polymer Science*, 138(43), 51284, 2021. https://doi.org/10.1002/ app.51284

Nurazzi N. M., Harussani M. M., Aisyah H. A., Ilyas R. A., Norrrahim M. N. F., Khalina A. and Abdullah N. Treatments of natural fiber as reinforcement in polymer composites – A short review. *Functional Composites and Structures*, 3(2), 024002, 2021. https://doi. org/10.1088/2631-6331/abff36

Pereira A. C., De Assis F. S., Garcia Filho F. D. C., Oliveira M. S., Lima E. S., Colorado Lopera H. A. and Monteiro S. N. Evaluation of the projectile's loss of energy in polyester composite reinforced with fique fiber and fabric. *Materials Research*, 22, 1–7, 2019. https://doi.org/10.1590/1980-5373-MR-2019-0146

Shalwan A. and Yousif B. F. In state of art: Mechanical and tribological behaviour of polymeric composites based on natural fibres. *Materials and Design*, 48, 14–24, 2013. https://doi. org/10.1016/j.matdes.2012.07.014

Suarez S. A., Gibson R. F., Sun C. T. and Chaturvedi S. K. The influence of fiber length and fiber orientation on damping and stiffness of polymer composite materials. *Experimental Mechanics*, 26(2), 175–184, 1986. https://doi.org/10.1007/BF02320012

Thomason J. L. and Vlug M. A. Influence of fibre length and concentration on the properties of glass fibre-reinforced polypropylene: 4. Impact properties. *Composites Part A: Applied Science and Manufacturing*, 28(3), 277–288, 1997. https://doi.org/10.1016/ S1359-835X(96)00127-3

Udaya Kiran C., Ramachandra Reddy G., Dabade B. M. and Rajesham S. Tensile properties of sun hemp, banana and sisal fiber reinforced polyester composites. *Journal of Reinforced Plastics and Composites*, 26(10), 1043–1050, 2007. https://doi.org/10.1177/073168440 7079423

3 Tribological Behavior of Sustainable Composites

3.1 INTRODUCTION

As indicated in the earlier chapters, the recent advances in the fabrication of different sustainable composites have motivated researchers to explore their use in the ever-demanding tribological applications. The ever-expanding horizon of the sustainable composites over the last few years has helped tribologists in particular to achieve the goals of a new emerging sub-field of tribology, namely the Green Tribology. The main goals of green tribology are to achieve energy conservation and environmental sustainability by the use of environmentally friendly materials, lubricants and processes. Thus, sustainable composites are an integral part of this exciting field whereby the use of natural fibers in developing composite materials with tailored mechanical, thermal and tribological properties would contribute to reducing the use of energy while minimizing the impact on the environment. Nosonovsky and Bhushan (2010) proposed the following twelve principles of green tribology:

1. Minimization of heat and energy dissipation
2. Minimization of wear
3. Reduction or complete elimination of lubrication and self-lubrication
4. Natural lubrication
5. Biodegradable lubrication
6. Sustainable chemistry and green engineering principles
7. Biomimetic approach
8. Surface texturing
9. Environmental implications of coatings
10. Design for degradation of surfaces
11. Real-time monitoring, analysis and control
12. Sustainable energy applications

Based on the twelve principles outlined above, the importance of sustainable composites in achieving the goals of green tribology cannot be overstated, and their use in demanding tribological applications such as the automobile and aerospace industries requires a thorough understanding of their wear and frictional behavior.

DOI: 10.1201/9781003270966-3

Thus, this chapter highlights the tribological performance of some sustainable composites in regard to reducing wear and friction in different applications.

3.2 SUSTAINABLE METALLIC COMPOSITES

Among the metals used for developing sustainable composites, aluminum and its alloys are some of the most commonly investigated for tribological applications due to their high strength to weight ratio, which will maximize energy conservation. Several natural fibers have been utilized to develop these aluminum sustainable composites, such as Rice husk ash, Spent tea leaves ash, Fly ash, Ground nut shell ash, Bamboo leaf ash, Breadfruit seed shell ash, Bagasse ash, Red mud, Melon shell ash, etc.,. To develop aluminum sustainable composites, several fabrication techniques have been used, such as powder metallurgy, stir casting and double stir casting. As shown in Figure 3.1 the metallic composites are fabricated using a variety of reinforcements, fabrication techniques and characterization techniques.

3.2.1 Fabrication Techniques of Metallic Sustainable Composites

Table 3.1 illustrates how various fabrication techniques, such as powder metallurgy, stir casting, double stir casting and compo casting, have been used to fabricate the metallic composites reinforced with natural fibers or particulates. For easy understanding, a short description of each technique is given below.

    a. **Powder Metallurgy**: This technique involves mixing the powders properly for preventing agglomeration of reinforcement particles in order to achieve uniform properties. This is usually carried out in a ball mill, using steel balls with a ball to powder weight ratio of 10:1. The powders are then compressed in a die using a press at a predetermined pressure to achieve good compaction without porosity after mixing. The green samples are then subsequently sintered in a tube furnace at a pre-determined temperature depending upon the metal matrix.

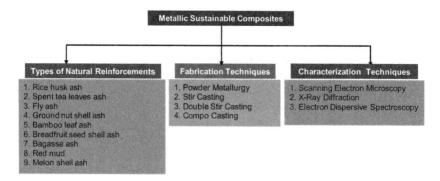

FIGURE 3.1 Various types of reinforcements, different fabrication techniques and characterization techniques used to manufacture and characterize the metallic composites.

TABLE 3.1

Summary of Tribological Characterization of Sustainable Metallic Composites

| Ref | Matrix Material/ Fabrication Technique | Reinforcement/ Loadings (wt.%) | Operating Conditions | | | Counter face | Remarks |
			Wear Test	Load (N)	Speed (m/s)		
Naim Shaikh et al. (2019)	Aluminum (Al)/Powder Metallurgy	Rice Husk Ash (RHA)/5, 10 15	Pin on disk	10, 20 30	1.5, 2.0, 2.5	EN- 32 steel disk	• Al reinforced with 10% RHA showed the best performance in terms of 16% increase in hardness and a 33% increase in wear resistance as compared to neat Al sample. • The addition of RHA particles changed the wear mechanism from abrasive to adhesive.
Naim Shaikh et al. (2019)	Aluminum (Al)/Powder Metallurgy	Spent Tea Leaves Ash (TLA)/1, 2, 3	Pin on disk	10, 20 30	1.5, 2.0, 2.5	EN32 steel	• Al reinforced with 2 wt.% TLA showed the best tribological performance in terms of increased hardness and increased wear resistance. • However, it was suggested that TLA can be used as a secondary reinforcement.

(continued)

TABLE 3.1 (Continued)
Summary of Tribological Characterization of Sustainable Metallic Composites

Ref	Matrix Material/ Fabrication Technique	Reinforcement/ Loadings (wt.%)	Operating Conditions			Counter face	Remarks
			Wear Test	Load (N)	Speed (m/s)		
Gladston et al. (2017)	Aluminum (Al)/ Compocasting	Rice Husk Ash (RHA)/2, 4, 6, 8	Pin on disk	10, 20 30, 40, 50	2	chromium steel disc	• RHA particles improved the wear resistance of the composites. • The improvement in wear resistance was attributed to increased hardness, generation of strain fields, homogenous distribution, spherical shape of RHA particles and reduction in effective contact area. • The wear mode transferred from adhesive to abrasive with increase in the content of RHA particles.
Dwiwedi et al. (2019)	Aluminum (Al6061)/Stir casting	Mussel Shell (MS)/ 2, 4, 6, 8, 10	Pin on disk	10, 20, 30	1	Steel	• Incorporation of MS particulates increased the overall hardness and wear resistance of composites with 6 wt.% demonstrating the best properties. • Coefficient of friction of composites decreased with an increase in load and sliding distance. • Wear mechanism shifted from mild to severe delamination with an increase in load.

Bannaravuri et al. (2018)	Al-4.5%Cu matrix/Stir Casting	Bamboo Leaf Ash (BLA)/2, 4, 6	Pin on disk	20, 30, 40	1.5, 2.0, 2.5	EN-32 steel	• The wear rate of the composites reduced with the addition of BLA particles. • A maximum reduction of 31.04% in wear rate was observed at 4 wt.% of BLA at an applied load of 20 N and a sliding velocity of 1.5 m/s. • Deep grooves were observed in the matrix alloy and, size and depth of the grooves reduced in the composite with an increase in BLA.
Razzaq et al. (2018)	AA6063 alloy/ Compo Casting	Fly Ash (FA)/2, 4, 6	Pin on disk	24.5, 49,73.5	150 rpm	EN32 steel	• The wear rate decreased with increasing weight content of FA reinforcements. • The wear rate decreased with increasing applied load.
Virkunwar et al. (2018)	Al6061/Stir Casting	Sugarcane Bagasse Ash (SCBA)/4, 8, 12 vol%	Pin on disk	19.62	3	EN8 steel	• Wear depth decreased with increase in volume fraction of SCBA reinforcement • Coefficient of friction increased with an increase in volume fraction up to 8vol % after which it reduced.
Alaneme et al. (2015)	Al-Mg-Si Alloy/ Two-step Stir Casting	Alumina/Graphite/ Rice husk ash (RHA) – 0, 25, 50, 75, 98.5	Tabor abrasion test	-	-	Abrasive wheel	• Hardness decreased with increase in the weight ratio of RHA and graphite in the composites; and with RHA content greater than 50%, the effect of graphite on the hardness becomes less significant.

(*continued*)

TABLE 3.1 (Continued)
Summary of Tribological Characterization of Sustainable Metallic Composites

Ref	Matrix Material/Fabrication Technique	Reinforcement/Loadings (wt.%)	Operating Conditions				Remarks
			Wear Test	Load (N)	Speed (m/s)	Counter face	
							• The composites without graphite exhibited greater wear susceptibility in comparison to the composite grades containing graphite. However, the wear resistance decreased with increase in the graphite content from 0.5 to 1.5 wt.%.
Manojkumar et al. (2016)	Al-6063 aluminum alloy/Stir Casting	Graphite (5, 10 15)/ Fly Ash (10)	Pin on disk	25, 50, 75	150, 300, 450 rpm	chromium steel disc	• A significant increase in the wear resistance was observed with the addition of fly ash and graphite. • Hybrid composite with 10% Fly ash and 5% of graphite showed the best performance in terms of low wear rate and low coefficient of friction.
Naim Shaikh et al. (2019)	Aluminum/Powder Metallurgy	SiC (10%)/Fly Ash (5, 10, 15)	Pin on disk	10, 20, 30	1.5, 2.0, 2.5	Steel	• The wear resistance of the composites increased with addition of the Fly ash particle content. The wear rate at 10 wt.% FA reinforced Al/SiC is reduced by 28% as compared to Al/SiC.

Tribological Behavior of Sustainable Composites 67

b. **Stir Casting**: This technique involves heating and melting the metallic matrix at its respective melting temperatures. The particulate reinforcing natural powder is also heated to remove all the absorbed moisture. The preheated reinforcing powder is added carefully in a controlled manner to the melt vortex created by the stirrer, set to rotate at a certain speed (usually 400 to 500 rpm) for a determined amount of time (usually 10 min). Thereafter, the molten alloy is cast in a preheated steel mold to produce samples of desired shapes.

c. **Double Stir Casting**: The double stir casting method is very much similar to the stir casting method except that the stirring is done in two steps. In the first step, the metallic matrix is heated to melting temperatures and melted, then cooled to a semi-solid state. The particulate reinforcing natural powder is also heated to remove all the absorbed moisture. The preheated reinforcing powder is added carefully in a controlled manner into the semi-solid metal matrix and is stirred manually for 10 minutes. Once this step is done, the mixture is then again super-heated to a temperature above the melting point of the metal matrix and is then mechanically stirred at a certain speed (usually 400 to 500 rpm) for a certain amount of time (usually 10 min). Afterwards, the molten alloy is cast in a preheated steel mold to produce samples of desired shapes.

d. **Compo Casting**: This technique is similar to the double stir casting process, which is also referred to as the compo casting technique. The procedure is similar to the one described under the double casting process.

3.2.2 Tribological Characterization of Metallic Sustainable Composites

Metals in general play an important role in industrial applications because of their excellent mechanical and thermal properties. However, to further improve their properties, efforts are being made to develop various types of metallic composites by reinforcing them with different types of fillers. Furthermore, to make these composites environmentally friendly, a shift from using synthetic fillers to natural fillers has been constantly taking place in the recent past, giving rise to the development of the metallic sustainable composites. Hence, to put these green composites to use in demanding tribological applications, it is very important to investigate and characterize their wear and friction properties. Table 1.6 of Chapter 1 presents the various configurations used to characterize the tribological properties of the sustainable composites. Further, Table 3.1 presents a bird's-eye view of the tribological characterization of developed aluminum sustainable composites for easy understanding.

3.2.3 Wear Mechanisms Observed in Metallic Sustainable Composites

Based on the analysis of wear tracks and wear debris generated during wear tests, two very important wear mechanisms, namely abrasive and adhesive, have been identified for the metallic composite reinforced with natural fibers and particles. It was observed that reinforcing aluminum with rice husk ash resulted in changing the wear mechanism from abrasive to adhesive/delamination, leading to a significant improvement in the wear resistance of the composites compared to pristine aluminum. Figure 3.2 shows the SEM micrographs of the wear track of aluminum composite reinforced with

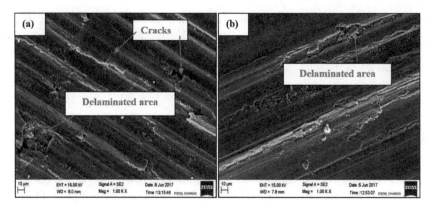

FIGURE 3.2 SEM micrograph of worn surface: (a) Al-4.5Cu/2BLA, (b) Al-4.5Cu/4BLA at L = 40 N and V = 3.5 m/s. (Bannaravuri et al. 2018)

bamboo leaf ash. A clear combination of deep grooves and delaminated areas coupled with some cracks can be seen, indicating a combination of abrasive wear by plastic deformation, micro-cutting, ploughing and delamination.

In general, a significant transition from severe abrasive wear to mild wear was observed in all the composites during the wear tests, especially compared to the neat metallic samples, where wear tracks were characterized by deep grooves, grain pullouts and micro cutting. Furthermore, with an increase in the applied load and speeds, a significant transition from mild to severe wear was observed for the composites as well.

3.3 SUSTAINABLE POLYMER COMPOSITES

Much research on Sustainable composites has been conducted on the tribological behavior and wear behavior of polymer composites (Singh et al. 2011). The various fabrication techniques of polymer sustainable composites have been discussed comprehensively in Table 1.3 of Chapter 1. Hence, this section mainly focuses on presenting and discussing the tribological performance of these composites in terms of wear and friction. Table 3.2 gives the summary of tribological behavior of some sustainable polymer composites.

As can be seen from Table 3.1 and Table 3.2, extensive research has been conducted in reinforcing metals and polymers with natural fibers to harness their advantages in developing sustainable green composites, which would contribute to the field of green tribology. Studies have been carried out to investigate the effect of different loadings of the fibers, the orientations of the fibers in the composite, as well as different operating conditions such as applied load and speed.

3.3.1 EFFECT OF FIBER ORIENTATIONS ON TRIBOLOGICAL PROPERTIES

Kenaf fiber reinforced composites were evaluated with respect to the sliding surface in three fiber orientations: normal, parallel and antiparallel (Singh et al. 2011). It

TABLE 3.2

List of Composites and Their COF and Wear under the Specified Conditions

Ref	Matrix Material	Reinforcement/ Loadings (wt.%)	Operating Conditions			Counter Face	Remarks
			Wear Test	Load (N)	Speed (m/s)		
Singh et al. (2011)	Polyurethane	Kenaf Fiber (KF)/25	Block on disk	50, 60, 70, 80	2.8	Stainless steel disk	• Treated KFRP composites performed better under higher applied loads. In other words, specific wear rates are lower at steady state under higher applied loads (70 and 80 N). • The predominant wear mechanisms under parallel and antiparallel contact conditions were plastic deformation and fiber tearing. • In normally oriented fibers, the wear mechanism was predominantly delamination caused by polymer swelling due to water absorption.
Chin and Yousif (2009)	Epoxy	Kenaf Fiber (KF)/48 vol%	Block on disk	30, 50, 70, 100	1.1 to 3.9	Stainless steel disk	• The fiber orientation had a significant influence on the frictional and wear performance of the composite. • The normally oriented kenaf fibers enhanced the wear performance of the epoxy by about 85% as compared to parallel and anti-parallel orientations. • The wear mechanisms of the composite were dominated by micro-cracks (in N-O) and debonding (in P-O) in the fibrous regions and deformation in the resinous regions.

(continued)

TABLE 3.2 (Continued)
List of Composites and Their COF and Wear under the Specified Conditions

Ref	Matrix Material	Reinforcement/ Loadings (wt.%)	Operating Conditions				Remarks
			Wear Test	Load (N)	Speed (m/s)	Counter Face	
Yousif and El-Tayeb (2007a)	Polyester	Oil Palm Fiber (OP)/45–48 vol%	Pin on disk	30, 50, 70, 100	1.7, 2.8, 3.9	Stainless steel disk	• A three to four fold enhancement in the wear resistance was observed in the OP reinforced polyester as compared to the neat matrix. • The wear mechanism of OPRP composite was predominated by debonding of fiber, bending of fiber, splitting the fiber bundles and polyester deformation. • A 5 to 23% reduction in the friction coefficient was observed when oil palm fiber was used as reinforcement for polyester.
Alajmi et al. (2021)	Epoxy	Bamboo fiber (BF)/	Block on disk	10, 15, 17, 20, 27, 32	1, 2, 3, 4	Steel	• Incorporation of BF significantly improved the tribological properties. • Coefficient of friction of the epoxy composites reduced significantly.
Ibrahim and Abdel-Barr (2013)	Polyester	Jasmine Leaves Particles (JLP)/ 5 to 50%	Pin on disk	2, 4, 6	1700 rpm	Steel	• Increasing the jasmine leaves in polyester composites significantly reduced the wear rates of the composites.

| Ibrahim (2016) | Polyester | Corn Straw Powder (CSP)/ 0 to 50% | Pin on disk | 2, 4, 6 | 1700 rpm | Steel | • The friction coefficient of the polyester composite increased with increasing the content of jasmine leaves particles at low loads.
• Polyester composites filled with jasmine leaves were recommended as high friction and low wear rate material for industrial applications such as brake linings.
• The friction coefficient of the composites decreased with the increasing content of corn straw in the polyester composites.
• Wear rate of polyester composites decreased to 0.005 g/min. with increase of corn straw contents to 40 wt.% |

was observed that the parallel orientation of the fibers results in lowest coefficient of friction (COF), whereas the normal orientation results in lowest wear rates of the composites. In normal orientation, the main wear mechanisms were delamination due to swelling caused by adsorption of water, fiber tearing and plastic deformations in antiparallel and parallel fiber orientations.

Other researchers also studied the behavior of kenaf fiber reinforced epoxy (KFRE) composites using epoxy matrix. Chin and Yousif (2009) tested the KFRE composites using a block-on-disk configuration at room temperature under varying loads, ranging from 30 N to 100 N. They also evaluated the effect of three different fiber orientations on tribological properties. The lowest COF and wear rates were achieved when the fibers were normally oriented; although the COF was around 0.52, it was still lower than some previous studies carried out by Hashmi et al (2007) on cotton fiber reinforced polyester composites, which reported COF of 0.6–1.

KFRE composites incorporating kenaf fibers improved their wearing performance by 85% when the fibers were oriented normal to the sliding direction, indicating that fiber inclination plays a significant role in wear and friction performances; however, the sliding velocity and applied load had no effect on the wear performance. The wear mechanisms were mainly microcracks in normally oriented fibers, debonding in the parallel fiber orientation and plastic deformation (Chin and Yousif 2009).

Yousif et al. (2007a) studied the behavior of oil palm fiber reinforced polyester composites (OPRFP) on a pin-on-disk machine, successfully reducing the friction and wear of the composites. The fibers were oriented randomly with the ends of fibers aligned normal to the sliding direction. They discovered that the specific wear rate increased with increasing sliding velocity regardless of the load, but remained steady after reaching 3 km of sliding distance. Compared to neat polyesters, the effect of the applied loads was less pronounced in OPRPs. Lower loads resulted in a higher specific wear rate that decreases with increasing applied loads.. In addition, the OPRP showed lower COF compared to neat polyesters; generally, the average COF decreases as the load increases.

Nirmal et al. (2012) investigated the adhesive wear behavior of Bamboo fiber reinforced epoxy composites (BFRE) using a pin-on-disk machine for three fiber orientations under dry sliding conditions. The best results were achieved in the anti-parallel orientation, but the other two orientations, parallel and random, achieved better results than neat composites. When the sliding speed was at 2.22 m/s, the anti-parallel oriented BFRE composites enhanced the specific wear rate by 60% compared to neat composites due to the increased high shear resistance of BFRE composites. The predominant wear mechanism for the three orientations was back film transfer.

3.3.2 EFFECT OF FIBER ORIENTATIONS AND TREATMENT ON THE TRIBOLOGICAL PROPERTIES

Goriparthi et al. (2012) studied the wear behavior of jute fiber reinforced composites. The surfaces of fibers were treated by silane treatment and other treatments to improve their mechanical properties. The fibers were oriented perpendicular to the sliding direction and the wear was calculated by reduction of mass. As the sliding distance

Tribological Behavior of Sustainable Composites

increased, the contact temperature increased, which may result in loosening of the bonding and increased wear. The treatment of the fibers improved the wear behavior by increasing the stiffness and interfacial adhesion.

3.3.3 EFFECT OF OPERATING CONDITIONS ON THE TRIBOLOGICAL PROPERTIES

Choudhary et al. (2018) evaluated the tribological performance of hemp fiber reinforced epoxy (HFRE) composites for different loads and sliding speeds under dry conditions. Compared to neat epoxy composites, the use of hemp fiber increased the COF of HFRE. For example, at 1 m/s and under a load of 30 N, the COF was 0.619 and 0.327 for HFRE and neat epoxy composites, respectively, and the increase in speed resulted in even higher COF. However, the wear performance enhanced at the sliding speed of 1 m/s and load of 10 N with a reduction of 29.06% in the specific wear rate. The predominant wear mechanisms were debonding, pullout and tearing of fibers.

Ibrahim (2016) evaluated the use of corn straw particles in polyester composites, concluding that the increase of corn straw content decreased the COF of polyester composites and reduced the wear rate after the corn straw content increased to 40 wt.% at which the wear rate is 0.005 g/min.

In addition, Ibrahim and Abdel-Barr (2013) investigated the behavior of polyester composites reinforced with jasmine leaves particles. Increasing the coarse particles content increased the COF of polyester composites under low loads. On the other hand, increasing the content of soft particles had remarkably decreased the wear rates of polyester composites. Therefore, polyester composites reinforced with jasmine leaves particles were recommended for high friction and low wear applications, such as brake linings.

3.3.4 WEAR MECHANISMS OBSERVED IN POLYMER SUSTAINABLE COMPOSITES

Several wear mechanisms such as cracking, material transfer, fiber pullout, debonding, ploughing and plastic deformation have been observed in various polymer sustainable composites. Chin and Yousif (2009) proposed different types of wear mechanisms in the composites reinforced with kenaf fiber oriented in different directions, as shown in Figure 3.3.

According to the proposed strategy, the sliding force with respect to the fiber orientation is one of the major factors in governing the wear damage of the composites. As can be seen from Figure 3.3 (a), fiber breakage or bending of the fibers can be considered as major wear mechanisms when the fibers are along the sliding direction, which is represented as the parallel orientation (P-O). Further, if the sliding force is in the anti-parallel direction (AP-O) to the fiber orientation, as shown in Figure 3.3 (b), the interfacial adhesion is sufficiently strong to prevent bending and/or debonding of fiber, but tear and breakage may still occur. And, if the sliding force is higher than the interfacial adhesion, debonding, bending and then detachment of the fibers could take place. Meanwhile, Figure 3.3 (c) shows what happens in the case of N-O when the ends of the fibers are exposed to the counterface. Since the fibers in the composite

74   Tribology in Sustainable Composites

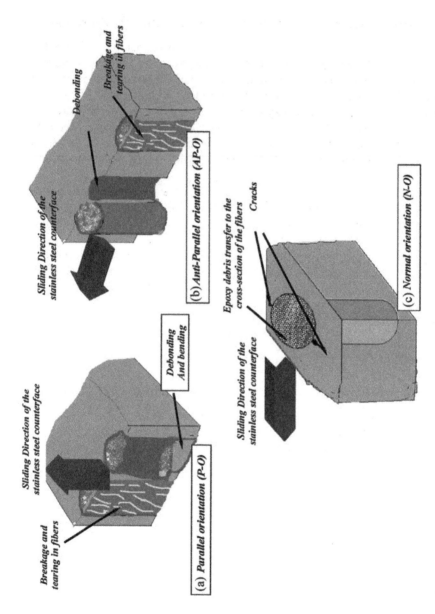

FIGURE 3.3 Proposed wear mechanism of the KFRE composite in three different orientations: (a) parallel orientation (P-O); (b) anti-parallel orientation (AP-O); (c) normal orientation (N-O). Chin and Yousif (2009)

Tribological Behavior of Sustainable Composites

are deeply embedded, detachment is not possible.. However, cracks may occur close to the fibers and perpendicular to the sliding direction due to the side shear force, Figure 3.3 (c). This can be further clarified by observing the worn surface of the composite.

3.4 COMPARISON OF THE TRIBOLOGICAL PROPERTIES OF A FEW POLYMER SUSTAINABLE COMPOSITES

Table 3.3 compares the specific wear rates and COF for a few combinations of fibers and polymer matrix available in literature, along with some remarks on the actual wear mechanisms observed.

TABLE 3.3

Comparison of Specific Wear Rates and Coefficients of Friction of a Few Combinations of Natural Fibers and Polymer Matrices Available in Literature

References	Fiber/Polymer Matrix	Range of Specific Wear Rates (x 10^{-5}) mm³/Nm	Range of Coefficients of Friction	Remarks
Chin and Yousif (2009)	Kenaf/Epoxy	0.15–2	0.52–0.68	Low wear, no pull-out or delamination of fibers
Hashmi et al. (2007)	Cotton/Polyester	0.1–6	0.6–1	Low wear, very high friction
Yousif and El-Tayeb (2007a)	Oil Palm/ Polyester	35–60	0.6–0.92	Moderate wear, high friction
Yousif and El-Tayeb (2007b)	Glass Fibers/ Polyester	0.2–0.6	0.4–0.6	Low wear, moderate friction
Tayeb (2008)	Sugarcane/ Polyester	5000–10000	0.02–0.25	Very high wear, low friction, pullout and delamination of fibers took place
El-Sayed et al. (1995)	Jute/Polyester	N/A	0.75–1	High friction

3.5 CONCLUSION AND FUTURE PROSPECTS

Recent years have seen an increase in tribological applications of sustainable composites. Sustainable composites due to their environmental-friendly properties are replacing the conventional composites. Based on published literature, there is much research in process to focus on the tribological behavior of sustainable composites using natural fiber-reinforced synthetic polymer matrix or resin. However, there is less research on the tribological behavior of sustainable metallic and ceramic composites. Most of the Metallic matrices used in the studies are aluminum. A further investigation of the tribological properties of completely sustainable ceramic composites is needed to understand the wear mechanism when compared with conventional composite materials. The use of natural fibers and particles to reinforce metallic matrices enhances their tribological behavior, leading to decreased wear rates and COF. The increase in particles volume reduces the wear rate and COF.

The tribological behavior of sustainable polymers composites is influenced by use of natural fibers and particles. The tribological performance of sustainable polymer composites improves when polymer composites are reinforced with natural fibers and particles compared to neat polymer composites. There is noticeable reduction in wear rate and COF during sliding, but they increase as the load increases. Furthermore, many studies concluded that the best fiber orientation with respect to sliding motion is the antiparallel orientation. The increase in sliding distance increases the contact interfacial temperature during sliding which increases the wear rate. The most predominant wear mechanisms are debonding, plastic deformation and tearing.

REFERENCES

Alajmi Eid A., Alotaibi J. G., Yousif B. F. and Nirmal U. Tribological studies of bamboo fibre reinforced epoxy composites using a BOD technique. *Polymers*, 13, 2444, 2021.

Alaneme K. K. and Sanusi K. O. Microstructural characteristics, mechanical and wear behaviour of aluminium matrix hybrid composites reinforced with alumina, rice husk ash and graphite. *Engineering Science and Technology, an International Journal*, 18(3), 416–422, 2015.

Bannaravuri P. K. and Birru A. K. Strengthening of mechanical and tribological properties of Al-4.5%Cu matrix alloy with the addition of bamboo leaf ash. *Results in Physics*, 10, 360–373, 2018.

Chaudhary V., Bajpai P. K. and Maheshwari, S. An Investigation on wear and dynamic mechanical behavior of jute/hemp/flax reinforced composites and its hybrids for tribological applications. *Fibers and Polymers*, 19, 403–415, 2018.

Chin C. W. and Yousif B. F. Potential of kenaf fibres as reinforcement for tribological applications. *Wear*, 267, 1550–1557, 2009.

Dwiwedi S. K., Srivastava A. K. and Chopkar M. Fabrication and dry sliding wear study of Al6061/mussel shell particulate composites, *SN Applied Sciences*, 1, 721, 2019.

El-Sayed A. A., El-Sherbiny M. G., Abo-El-Ezz A. S. and Aggag G. A. Friction and wear properties of polymeric composite materials for bearing applications. *Wear*, 184(1), 45–53, 1995.

El-Tayeb N. S. M. A study on the potential of sugarcane fibers/polyester composite for tribological applications. *Wear*, 265(1–2), 223–235, 2008.

Tribological Behavior of Sustainable Composites

Gladston J. A. K., Dinaharan I., Sheriff N. Mohd. and Selvam J. D. R. Dry sliding wear behavior of AA6061 aluminum alloy composites reinforced rice husk ash particulates produced using compocasting. *Journal of Asian Ceramic Societies*, 5(2), 127–135, 2017.

Goriparthi B. K., Suman K. N. S. and Rao N. M. Effect of fiber surface treatments on mechanical and abrasive wear performance of polylactide/jute composites. *Composites Part A: Applied Science and Manufacturing*, 43(10), 1800–1808, 2012.

Hashmi S. A. R., Dwivedi U. K. and Chand N. Graphite modified cotton fibre reinforced polyester composites under sliding wear conditions. *Wear*, 262(11–12), 1426–1432, 2007.

Ibrahim R. A., Influence of natural fillers on tribological and mechanical performance of polyester composites. *Journal of the Egyptian Society of Tribology*, 13(1), 43–53, 2016.

Ibrahim R. A. and Abdel-Barr M. M. Tribological and mechanical performance of polyester composites filled by jasmine dry leaves. *Journal of the Egyptian Society of Tribology*, 10(4), 58–65, 2013.

Manojkumar M. and Shanmuga Prakash R. Wear characteristics of hybrid Al 6063 matrix composites reinforced with graphite and fly ash particulates. *Applied Mechanics and Materials*, 854, 1–9, 2016.

Naim Shaikh Mohd. B. A statistical analysis of wear behaviour of fly ash reinforced al-sic hybrid composites. *Journal of Powder Metallurgy & Mining*, 7(1), 190, 2019.

Nirmal U., Hashim J. and Low K. O. Adhesive wear and frictional performance of bamboo fibres reinforced epoxy composite. *Tribology International*, 47, 122–133, 2012.

Nosonovsky M. and Bhushan B. Green tribology: principles, research areas and challenges, *Philosophical Transactions of Royal Society A*. 3684677–3684694. 2010. http://doi.org/10.1098/rsta.2010.0200

Razzaq A. Mohd. and Dayang L. M. Effect of fly ash content and applied load on wear behaviour of AA6063 aluminium alloy. *IOP Conference Series: Materials Science and Engineering*, 429, 012038, 2018.

Shaikh Mohd B. N. and Ali Mohd. Microstructural, mechanical and tribological behaviour of aluminium matrix composites reinforced with spent tea leaves ash. *Materials Focus*, 7, 1–7, 2018.

Shaikh Mohd B. N., Raja S., Ahmed M., Zubair Mohd, Khan A. and Ali Mohd. Rice husk ash reinforced aluminium matrix composites: Fabrication, characterization, statistical analysis and artificial neural network modelling. *2019 Materials Research Express*, 6, 056518, 2019.

Singh N., Yousif B. F. and Rilling D. Tribological characteristics of sustainable fiber-reinforced thermoplastic composites under wet adhesive wear. *Tribology Transactions*, 54(5), 736–748, 2011.

Virkunwar A. K., Ghosh S. and Basak R. Study of mechanical and tribological characteristics of aluminium alloy reinforced with sugarcane bagasse ash, an international conference on tribology, *TRIBOINDIA-2018 13th–15th December 2018*, VJTI, Mumbai, India.

Yousif B. F. and El-Tayeb N. S. M. The effect of oil palm fibers as reinforcement on tribological performance of polyester composite. *Surface Review and Letters*, 14(6), 1095–1102, 2007a.

Yousif B. F. and El-Tayeb N. S. M. Tribological evaluations of polyester composites considering three orientations of CSM glass fibers using BOR machine. *Applied Composite Materials*, 14(2), 105–116, 2007b.

4 Applications of Sustainable Composites

4.1 INTRODUCTION

The growing concern over the environment has caused a call to replace synthetic fibers with their natural counterparts in composite materials in order to make them more sustainable. However, due to some fundamental limitations, such as high cost, durability, bonding integrity and a gap in the development of standards among others, the use of natural fiber reinforced composites is restricted in demanding applications. Nevertheless, due to the technological advancements and the in-roads made by extensive research in this area industries have now started to adopt sustainable composites in various applications in a more efficient manner. Historically, sustainable composite materials have been used in many commercial applications. Bamboo shoot particles, for example, were used by ancient civilizations in the construction of mud walls and laminated glued wood by Egyptians in 1500 BCE. The metals were laminated for making swords (1800 AD). Further, as time moved forward, various materials were developed as per the requirement of industries. The innovation of materials as per the requirement of civilization is presented in Figure 4.1. The sustainable materials are slowly growing and being adopted by the industries in the 21st century because of their biodegradable and renewable properties.

Furthermore, the rapid industrialization over the past few decades and its excessive impact on the environment has put tremendous pressure on governments worldwide to introduce green/sustainable composites rapidly, which in turn has led researchers to look for ways and means to replace synthetic fibers with natural ones. Natural fibers with their inherent advantages of recyclability and biodegradability along with a wide range of mechanical and thermal properties are an excellent alternative to counter the disadvantages of the synthetic fibers. However, a balance of social, economic and environmental factors has to be considered for their effective application in various industries. Figure 4.2 presents a summary of the factors to be considered while developing sustainable composites.

Hence based upon viability, sustainable composites especially the natural fiber based polymer composites are increasingly replacing other materials in various industries/applications such as food, agriculture, medical, automotive, aerospace and energy, to name a few. The following sections describe in detail the scope of use of sustainable composites in the above-mentioned industries/applications.

DOI: 10.1201/9781003270966-4

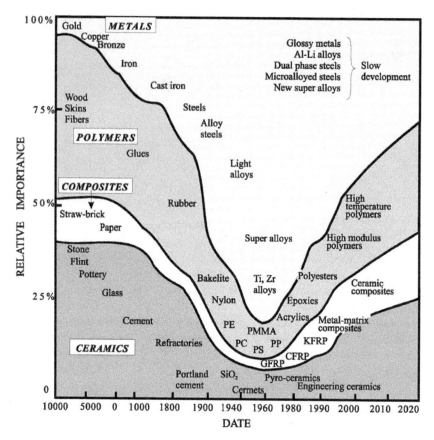

FIGURE 4.1 Progression of materials with respect to time as per the requirement of civilization. (Ashby et al. 1987)

Furthermore, it is very important to choose an appropriate polymer matrix for the development of sustainable products. Polymer is a material consisting of a single or many repeating chains of molecules. It can be arranged in two ways: randomly or unidirectionally, resulting in crystalline and amorphous structures, respectively. These are divided into two major groups: thermosets and thermoplastic. The molecules of thermosets are tightly cross-linked and covalently bonded, which makes it tough and wear resistant, whereas the molecules of thermoplastics are weakly bonded with van der Waals forces and are used to develop composites for locations that need both weaker and stronger mechanical properties (Yao et al. 2018). Among both polymers, thermosets are widely used to develop structures with improved thermal stability, creep and chemical resistance, ease of processing and good wetting properties (Gouzman et al. 2019). Therefore, it is necessary to understand the properties of polymers for appropriate applications. Table 4.1 summarizes the properties of different polymer matrices used in the development of a sustainable product.

Applications of Sustainable Composites

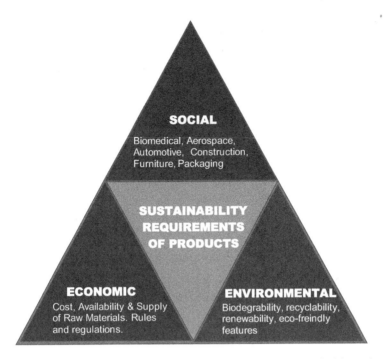

FIGURE 4.2 Different factors to be considered prior to developing sustainable products.

TABLE 4.1
Properties of Different Polymer Matrices

Polymer	Density (g/cm³)	Tensile Strength (MPa)	Tensile Modulus (MPa)	Melting Temperature (°C)	Thermal Conductivity (W·m⁻¹·K⁻¹)	Total Heat Release (kJ/g)
Polyethylene	0.93	15	0.8	105–115	0.33–0.51	41.6
Polypropylene	0.92	40	1.9	130	0.1–0.2	41.4
Polyacrylonitrile	1.18	57	2.7	300	1.0	13.3
Polycarbonates	1.2	70	2.6	157	0.19	20.3
Polystyrene	1.1	40	3	240	0.03	38.8
Polymethyl methacrylate	1.18	47	2.2	130	0.20	24.3
Polyvinyl chloride	1.4	51	2.4	160	0.19	11.3
Polyvinyl acetate	1.19	40	1.7	200	0.31	21.6
Polylactic acid	1.2–1.4	50	3.5	150–160	1.13	14.2
Polyethylene terephthalate	1.38	55	2.7	260	0.15	15.3

Source: Syduzzaman et al. 2020.

4.2 APPLICATIONS OF SUSTAINABLE COMPOSITES

Sustainable composites find usage in a broad range of civil and mechanical engineering applications in automobile, aerospace, food, agriculture, construction and biomedical industries.

4.2.1 SUSTAINABLE COMPOSITES IN CIVIL STRUCTURES

Natural fiber reinforced sustainable composites have been making inroads into numerous civil engineering applications. Qualities such as light weight, chemical resistance, corrosion resistance, ability to be molded to any shape, can be processed using existing technology, environmental friendliness and sustainability have made them an ideal candidate for these applications. Bio-based composites for roof structures in the form of paper sheets were fabricated from cellulose fibers and soy oil-based resins. These were found to possess excellent strength and stiffness essential for roof construction (Dweib et al. 2006). Panels with a density of 0.7 g/cm^3 were fabricated with sunflower stalk fiber contents of 25, 50 and 75%, and were found to have excellent properties for use as particleboards (Bektas et al. 2005). Wood fibers/ plastic composites have been used in large quantities for applications in window, doorframes, decks, docks and molded panel components (John and Thomas 2008; Li and Matuana 2003; Owonubi et al. 2018). Natural fiber composites are replacing asbestos in the construction industry because of the health challenges asbestos poses (Coutts 2005). Architecture is one of the fields where the natural fiber reinforced composites have a bright future as they are being used to fabricate a variety of building materials for sunscreens, cladding, walling, flooring, etc. (Steffens et al. 2017).

4.2.2 SUSTAINABLE COMPOSITES IN AUTOMOBILE INDUSTRY

In the US alone, an approximated mass of 20 million automobile plastic parts, such as bumpers, finds its way into landfill each year (Peijs 2003). Even Australia contributes about 1.3 million damaged automotive plastic parts worth approximately $ 260 million, and weighing about 3,000 tons, to the landfills every year (Peijs 2003). This excessive plastic land filling all over the world has a potential to create a very harmful impact on the environment. Hence, many governments around the globe have started making concerted efforts in protecting the environment by striving to reduce the waste generated from different products, which have a harmful effect on the carbon footprint, in general. For instance, "end of life vehicle (ELV)" regulations, implemented by the European Union in 2010 projected reduction in final waste when disposing an EVL to 5% by year 2015. In the adopted regulations, it is very clearly stated that 85% of material used in the manufacture of a vehicle must be reusable or recyclable mechanically (John and Thomas 2008; McDonagh 2004), which has increased interest in natural fiber reinforced sustainable composites.

Because of the high durability of natural fiber reinforced polymer composites and the available technologies for their fabrication, various automotive parts can now be manufactured in large and complex shapes, making them very popular in the automotive industry (Dunne et al. 2016; Bos 2004; Brief 2011). Hence, automotive

Applications of Sustainable Composites 83

manufacturers all over the world have started utilizing renewable composite materials to manufacture various components of a vehicle. These sustainable composites have a number of benefits for automotive manufacturers: they are biodegradable/renewable by nature, eco-friendly, help achieve fuel efficiency through their lighter weight and provide good mechanical, acoustic and thermal properties (Komornicki et al. 2015). Hence globally, the use of renewable composites has been steadily increasing in the automotive industry. According to a few statistics, in Brazil alone, automobile industries use, on average, 10–12.7 kg of natural fiber reinforcement per vehicle for the fabrication of parts, such as rear door liners, front doors, boot liners, parcel shelves, sunroof interior shields and headrests (Dunne et al. 2016). Natural fibers such as flax, hemp, sisal and wool have also been used in Mercedes-Benz components (Holbery and Houston 2006). Furthermore, consistent efforts are being made by automotive manufacturers to increase the use of natural fiber reinforced composites in various interior and exterior parts of a vehicle (Shuit et al. 2009; Mohammed et al. 2015)

Although sustainable composites have gained tremendous interest in the automotive industry, a few challenges remain before the synthetic fibers are completely replaced by their natural counterparts (La Mantia et al. 2011; Marsh 2003; La Mantia et al. 2006; Netravali and Chabba 2003). The sustainable composites present several complex challenges for scientists and engineers in order to meet the high level of service and production specifications of the automotive sector. To overcome these challenges and provide sustainability to the renewable composite material, three main strategies are used: (1) to improve the properties of the selected material (Urry 1995; Girotti et al. 2004), (2) to formulate adequate compounding and reinforcement (Ammar et al. 2006) and (3) to develop design and processing methods that are more adapted to the behavior and properties of these materials (Divya et al. 2016). Syduzzaman et al. (2020) have summarized the application of NFRCs in automotive industry as shown in Table 4.2.

4.2.3 Sustainable Composites in Medical Industry

In olden days, the natural materials (wood, glue and rubber, and tissues from living organs) and manufactured materials (iron, gold, zinc and glass) were used as biomaterials on the basis of trial and error. In some cases, the body accepts materials but in some cases the body does not accept materials. It depends on the interaction of tissues with materials. In the past 30 years, researchers have obtained considerable progress to understand the interaction of tissue and materials. Further, they are able to differentiate between living and non-living materials. Due to this understanding, they have invented the word Biocompatibility and Biomaterials (Williams 1988). The term biocompatibility is defined as the harmony of material with living organs. Further, this term is extended and differentiates between surface and structural compatibility (Wintermantel and Mayer 1995). Surface compatibility refers to the chemical, physical and biological means, whereas structural compatibility refers to the mechanical properties of materials. Therefore, it is important to know the factors required for proper selection of biomaterials in medical industry. These are shown in Table 4.3.

TABLE 4.2
Application of NFRCs in Automotive Industry

Car Manufacturer	Model	Application Areas
Rover	2000 and others	Insulations, rear storage panel
Audi	A2, A3, A4, A6, A8	Seatback, side and back door panel, spare-tire lining, boot-liner
Opel	Astra, Vectra, Zafira	Head-liner panel, door panels, instrumental panel
BMW	3, 5 and 7 series	Head-liner panel, seatback, door panel, car dashboard
Toyota	Raum, Harrier, Brevis	Floor mats, door panels, spare tire cover
Mercedes Ben	C, S, E and A classes	Door panel, glove box, seat backrest panel, trunk panel, sun visor, roof cover
Volkswagen	Bora, Golf, A4	Door panel, seatback, boot-liner
Peugeot	406	Parcel shelf, seatback, door panels
Fiat	Brava, Punto, Marea	Door panels
Volvo	V70, C70	Cargo floor tray, seat padding
Ford	Focus	Floor trays, door inserts, door panels, boot-liner
Mitsubishi	---	Door panels, instrumental panels
Citroen	C5	Interior door paneling
Renault	Twingo, Cilo	Rear parcel shelf

Source: Syduzzaman et al. 2020.

TABLE 4.3
Important Factors for Selection of Biomaterials in Medical Application

Factors	Description		
1st Level material properties	Chemical/biological characteristics Chemical composition (Bulk and surface)	Physical characteristics Density	Mechanical/structural characteristics Elastic modulus Poisson's ratio Yield strength Tensile strength Compressive strength
2nd Level material properties	Adhesion	Surface topology (texture and roughness)	Hardness Shear modulus Shear strength Flexural modulus Flexural strength

Applications of Sustainable Composites 85

TABLE 4.3 (Continued)
Important Factors for Selection of Biomaterials in Medical Application

Factors	Description		
Specific functional requirements (based on application)	Bio-functionality (non-thrombogenic, cell adhesion, etc.) Bio-inert (non-toxic, non-irritant, non-allergic, non-carcinogenic, etc.) Bioactive Bio-stability (resistant to corrosion, hydrolysis, oxidation, etc.) Biogradation	Form (solid, porous, coating, film, fiber, mesh, powder) Geometry Coefficient of thermal expansion Electrical conductivity Color, aesthetics Refractive index Opacity or translucency	Stiffness or rigidity Fracture toughness Fatigue strength Creep resistance Friction and wear resistance Adhesion strength Impact strength Proof stress Abrasion resistance
Processing and fabrication	Reproducibility, quality, sterilizability, packaging, secondary processability		
Characteristics of host: Tissue, organ, species, age, sex, race, health condition, activity, systemic response Medical/surgical procedure, period of application/usage Cost			

Source: Ramakrishna et al. 2001.

Moreover, in 21st century, the sustainable composites with their numerous advantages in terms of properties, biodegradability, etc. find a variety of applications in the medical industry. A wide range of sustainable composites finds usage in different applications such as fabrication of artificial bone, spine instrumentation, knee/hip replacement and bone cementing. They are also used for soft tissue replacements and implantations, such as ureter prosthesis, catheters, vascular grafts, tendons and ligaments instead of conventional metal alloy and ceramic. Figure 4.3 gives an excellent summary of the usage of sustainable composites for different applications in the human body. Furthermore, it was observed that numerous patents were registered using natural fibers for biomedical application. The summarized data is shown in Table 4.4.

4.2.4 SUSTAINABLE COMPOSITES FOR ENERGY APPLICATIONS

It was found in Global Wind Energy Council (GWEC) report that there are more than 3 million wind turbines installed throughout the world. They are designed in a manner that they have a life span of ~20 years. But the recycling of retired turbine

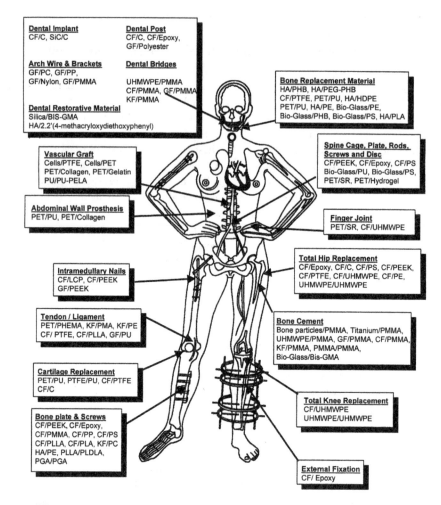

FIGURE 4.3 Various applications of different green polymer composites in human prosthesis. (Ramakrishna et al. 2001)

blades is a major issue nowadays. To overcome disposal of these blades, most of the European countries have now banned the use of traditional composite materials. As a result, scientists have developed an alternative known as sustainable composite material, which has superior properties, is renewable and is ecofriendly. Sustainable composites were first used in the development of turbine blades (Debnath et al. 2013) due to their excellent properties such as high strength, low cost, eco-friendly

Applications of Sustainable Composites

TABLE 4.4

The Summarized Registered Patent Data of Natural Fiber for Biomedical Application

S. No.	Patent Title	Patent Number	Year
1	Surface treated biocomposite material, medical implants comprising same and methods of treatment thereof	US10869954B2	2020
2	Anisotropic biocomposite material, medical implants comprising same and methods of treatment thereof	AU2015310510B2	2020
3	Fiber reinforced biocomposite medical implants with high mineral content	WO2018002917A1	2018
4	Medical balloon with incorporated fibers	W0/2013/148399	2013
5	Polyester cool-fiber antibacterial pillow	CN102715804	2012
6	Medical natural porous fiber filler and vacuum sealing drainage device thereof	CN102715983	2012
7	Manufacturing process of antibacterial bamboo pulp used for high-wet-modulus fiber	CN102677504	2012
8	Flushable moist wipe or hygiene tissue	CN102665510-	2012
9	Far-infrared fiber fabric functional bellyband by utilizing nano-selenium, germanium and zinc elements traditional Chinese medicine	CN101703317	2010
10	Medical device for insertion into a joint	US20090234459	2008
11	Medical device for insertion into a joint	EU1896088	2008
12	Antiviral fiber and producing method and use thereof	CN1609336	2006
13	Manufacturing of nano-fibers, from natural fibers, agro based fibers and root fibers	CA2437616	2005
14	Natural antibacterial material and its use	CN461827	2003
15	Absorbable protective coatings for wound with the use of sponge and process for producing the same	W0/20021054998	2006
16	Medical prosthesis, especially for aneurysms, with a connection between its liner and its structure	EPOB18184	1998

Source: Namvar et al. 2014; Preiss-Bloom and LINDNER 2020 and 2018; LINDER and Preiss-Bloom 2020.

and lightweight. Moving forward, recycling will be more demanding in 2020s. Presently ~80–90% of total mass of wind turbines can be recycled. It is also noticed that wind energy division worldwide utilizes ~2.5 million composite materials. Therefore, in wind energy industry, the sustainable composites will play a very vital role worldwide.

TABLE 4.5
Specific Capacitance of Green Supercapacitors Electrode Materials

Green Material	Specific Capacitance (Fg^{-1})
Conjugated polymer	105–587
Synthetic co-polymer	145–268.5
Cellulose	70–380
Doped cellulose	>100–300
Starch	160–304
Gelatin	183
Carbohydrate	210–300

Source: Kausar 2021.

Thereafter, sustainable composites were used in optoelectronic industry. Moving forward, the green polymers were used in light emitting diode devices (LED). In addition, these green conducting polymers were used in photovoltaic industries. The insertion of green fillers in p-type conjugated polymer may acquire donor-acceptor structure for photo energy conversion. It is noticed that the use of green composites improves the steadfastness and eco-friendliness (Zhuang et al. 2015). Further, a few attempts were made to develop green electrode based supercapacitors using sustainable materials (Mensah-Darkwa et al. 2019) for high flexibility, better specific capacitance and recyclability. Table 4.5 shows the specific capacitance of different green supercapacitors (Kausar 2021). Therefore, it can be concluded that the sustainable composites have prominent materials in different areas of energy sectors due to its biodegradability and renewable property.

4.2.5 Sustainable Composites for Miscellaneous Applications

In addition to the major industries such as the civil/structures, automobile/aerospace and biomedical mentioned above, sustainable composites find their usage in numerous other miscellaneous applications. They have been implemented in applications such as blowing insulation, pouring insulation, impact sound insulation materials and ceiling panels for thermal insulation, and acoustic soundproofing (Akin 2010). The flax fibers were used in the manufacturing of GreenBente24 boat (Ticoalu et al. 2010). Rice husk fiber, cotton, ramie, jute fiber, kenaf are used in various applications like furniture industry, clothing, ropes, sewing thread, fishing nets, packing materials and paper manufacture (Thyavihalli Girijappa et al. 2019). The coir/polyester-reinforced composites were used in mirror casings, paperweights, voltage stabilizer covers, projector covers, helmets and roofs (Khondker et al. 2005).

Further, it was found that nanofiber composite materials were suitable for a range of different environmental friendly applications, including batteries, environmental awareness, superhydrophobicity, superhydrophilicity, superconductivity, and

Applications of Sustainable Composites

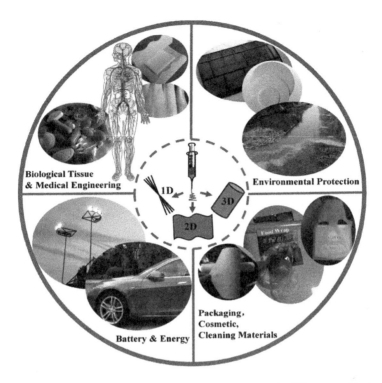

FIGURE 4.4 Application of nanofibers sustainable composites in different applications. (Liu et al. 2020)

adjustable mechanical properties, biological tissue and medical engineering, as well as food packaging and cosmetic materials. They can absorb pollutants from air and water because of their large surface area and extraordinary porosity. Nanofiber composites are manufactured using electrospinning technology, for which they are also known as electrospun sustainable composites (Liu et al. 2020). Nanofibers can be assembled in the form of 1D, 2D and 3D structures. Their relative applications are shown in Figure 4.4.

4.3 SUMMARY

Due to the ever-increasing awareness to protect the environment from the harmful effects of synthetic materials and the regulations being introduced by different governments around the world, many industries are turning to natural fibers for fabricating composite materials. Given the advantages of biodegradability, recyclability and renewability of natural fibers, they are excellent candidates for replacing synthetic fibers. However, these natural fibers, which are usually extracted from plants and animals, also suffer from certain limitations such as poor resistance to moisture and incompatibility with the matrix material. Therefore, it is critical to improve these properties before using them in demanding applications for achieving better efficiency and performance. However, it is to be noted that, given the outlook of the global economies towards making a green environment, the natural fiber is here to stay and will become one of the indispensable sustainable and renewable resources in the field of composites which can replace synthetic fibers in many applications.

REFERENCES

Akin D. E. Chemistry of plant fibres, in *Industrial Applications of Natural Fibres: Structure, Properties and Technical Applications*, ed. J. Müssing (West Sussex: John Wiley & Sons Ltd.), 13–22, 2010.

Ammar I., Cheikh R. B., Compos A. R. and Cunha A. M. Injection molded composites of short Alfa fibers and biodegradable blends. *Polymer Composite*, 27(4), 341–348, 2006.

Ashby M., Bush S. F., Swindells N., Bullough R., Ellison G., Lindblom Y., Cahn R. W. and Barnes J. F. Technology of the 1990s: Advanced materials and predictive design [and discussion]. *Philosophical Transactions of the Royal Society A*, 322, 393–407, 1987.

Bektas I., Guler C., Kalaycioğlu H., Mengeloglu F. and Nacar M. The manufacture of particleboards using sunflower stalks (Helianthus annuus L.) and poplar wood (Populus alba L.). *Journal of Composite Materials*, 39(5), 467–473, 2005.

Bos H. L. *The Potential of Flax Fibres as Reinforcement for Composite Materials* (Eindhoven: Technische Universiteit Eindhoven), 2004.

Brief L. *Opportunities in Natural Fiber Composites* (Irving (TX): Lucintel LLC), 2011.

Coutts R. S. A review of Australian research into natural fibre cement composites. *Cement and Concrete Composites*, 27(5), 518–526, 2005.

Debnath K., Singh I. and Dvivedi A., Kumar P. Natural fibre-reinforced polymer composites for wind turbine blades: Challenges and opportunities, in *Recent Advances in Composite Materials for Wind Turbine Blades,* ed. A. Brahim (Hong Kong, China: WAP-AMSA), 25–40, 2013.

Divya G. S. and Suresha B. Recent developments of natural fiber reinforced thermoset polymer composites and their mechanical properties. *Indian Journal of Advances in Chemical Science*, S1, 267–274, 2016.

Dunne R., Desai D., Sadiku R. and Jayaramudu J. A review of natural fibres, their sustainability and automotive applications. *Journal of Reinforced Plastics and Composites*, 35(13), 1041–1050, 2016.

Dweib M., Hu B., Shenton H. III and Wool R. Bio-based composite roof structure: Manufacturing and processing issues. *Composite Structures*, 74(4), 379–388, 2006.

Girotti, A., Reguera, J., Rodríguez-Cabello, J. C. et al. Design and bioproduction of a recombinant multi(bio)functional elastin-like protein polymer containing cell adhesion sequences for tissue engineering purposes. *Journal of Materials Science: Materials in Medicine*, 15, 479–484, (2004). https://doi.org/10.1023/B:JMSM.0000021 124.58688.7a

Gouzman I., Atar N., Grossman E., Verker R., Bolker A., Pokrass M., Sultan S., Sinwani O., Wagner A. and Lück T. 3D printing of bismaleimides: From new ink formulation to printed thermosetting polymer objects. *Advanced Materials Technologies*, 4, 1900368, 2019.

Holbery J. and Houston D. Natural-fiber-reinforced polymer composites in automotive applications. *The Journal of The Minerals, Metals & Materials Society,* 58, 80–86, 2006.

John M. J. and Thomas S. Biofibres and biocomposites. *Carbohydrate Polymers*, 71(3), 343–364, 2008.

Kausar A. Green Nanocomposites for Energy Storage. *Journal of Composites Science*, 5, 202, 2021.

Applications of Sustainable Composites

Khondker O. A., Ishiaku U. S., Nakai A. and Hamada H. Fabrication and mechanical properties of unidirectional jute/PP composites using jute yarns by film stacking method. *Journal of Polymers and the Environment,* 13, 115–126, 2005.

Komornicki J., Bax L., Vasiliadis H. and Ong K. Polymer composites for automotive sustainability. *Innovation Manager and SusChem Secretary,* 2015.

La Mantia F. and Morreale M. Green composites: A brief review. *Composites Part A: Applied Science and Manufacturing,* 42(6), 579–588, 2011.

La Mantia F. and Morreale M. Mechanical properties of recycled polyethylene ecocomposites filled with natural organic fillers. *Polymer Engineering & Science,* 46(9), 1131–1139, 2006.

Li Q. and Matuana L. M. Surface of cellulosic materials modified with functionalized polyethylene coupling agents. *Journal of Applied Polymer Science,* 88(2), 278–286, 2003.

Linder T. P. and Preiss-Bloom O. *Surface Treated Biocomposite Material, Medical Implants Comprising Same and Methods of Treatment Thereof,* US Patent, Patent Number: US10869954B2, 2020.

Liu H., Gough C. R., Deng Q., Gu Z., Wang F. and Hu X. Recent advances in electrospun sustainable composites for biomedical, environmental, energy, and packaging applications. *International Journal of Molecular Sciences,* 21, 4019, 2020.

Marsh G. Next step for automotive materials. *Materials Today,* 6(4), 36–43, 2003.

McDonagh G. Automotive plastic waste: Volumes entering landfill in Australia and a strategy for reduction. Diss. Thesis from the University of South Australia, 2004.

Mensah-Darkwa K., Zequine C., Kahol P. K. and Gupta, R. K. Supercapacitor energy storage device using biowastes: A sustainable approach to green energy. *Sustainability,* 11, 414, 2019.

Mohammed L., Ansari M. N. M., Pua G., Jawaid M. and Islam M. S. A review on natural fiber reinforced polymer composite and its applications. *International Journal of Polymer Science,* 2015, 1–15, 2015.

Namvar F., Jawaid M., Md Tahir P., Mohamad R., Azizi S., Khodavandi A., Rahman H. S. and Nayeri M. D. Potential use of plant fibres and their composites for biomedical applications. *BioResources,* 9(3), 5688–5706, 2014.

Netravali A. N. and Chabba S. Composites get greener. *Materials Today,* 4(6), 22–29, 2003.

Owonubi S. J., Linganiso L. Z., Motaung T. E. and Songca S. P. Wood and its byproducts: Cascading utilisation for biomass (re)generation, in *"Waste-to Profit" (W-t-P): Circular Economy in the Construction Industry for a Sustainable Future,* eds. L. Z. Linganiso and T. E. Motaung (United States of America: Nova Publishers), 293–311, 2018.

Peijs T. Composites for recyclability. *Materials Today,* 4(6), 30–35, 2003.

Preiss-Bloom O. and Linder T. P., *Anisotropic Biocomposite Material, Medical Implants Comprising Same and Methods of Treatment Thereof,* Australian Patent, Patent Number: AU2015310510B2, 2020.

Preiss-Bloom O. and Linder T. P., *Fiber Reinforced Biocomposite Medical Implants with High Mineral Content,* Patent Number: WO2018002917A1, 2018.

Ramakrishna S., Mayer J., Wintermantel E. and Leong K. W. Biomedical applications of polymer-composite materials: A review, *Composites Science and Technology,* 61, 1189–1224, 2001.

Reguera G. J., Rodriguez-Cabello J., Arias F., Alonso M. and Testera A. Design and bioproduction of a recombinant multi(bio)functional elastin-like protein polymer containing cell adhesion sequences for tissue engineering purposes. *Journal of Materials Science: Materials in Medicine,* 15, 479–484, 2004.

Shuit S. H., Tan K. T., Lee K. T. and Kamaruddin A. H. Oil palm biomass as a sustainable energy source: A Malaysian case study. *Energy,* 34, 1225–1235, 2009.

Steffens F., Steffens H. and Oliveira F. R. Applications of natural fibers on architecture. *Procedia Engineering*, 200, 317–324, 2017.

Syduzzaman Md., Al Faruque A. Md., Bilisik K. and Naebe M. Plant-based natural fibre reinforced composites: A review on fabrication. *Properties and Applications, Coatings*, 10, 973, 2020.

Thyavihalli Girijappa Y. G., Mavinkere Rangappa S., Parameswaranpillai J. and Siengchin S. Natural fibers as sustainable and renewable resource for development of eco-friendly composites: A comprehensive review. *Frontiers in Materials,* 6, 226, 2019.

Ticoalu A., Aravinthan T. and Cardona F. A review of current development in natural fiber composites for structural and infrastructure applications, in *Southern Region Engineering Conference 11–12 November 2010,* Toowoomba, Australia, 1–5, 2010.

Urry Dan W. Elastic biomolecular machines. *Scientific American,* 272(1), 64–69, 1995.

Williams D. F. Consensus and definitions in biomaterials, in *Advances in Biomaterials*, eds. C. de Putter, K. de Lange, K. de Groot and A. J. C. Lee (Amsterdam: Elsevier Science), 11–16, 1988.

Wintermantel E. and Mayer J. Anisotropic biomaterials strategies and developments for bone implants, in *Encyclopedic Handbook of Biomaterials and Bioengineering, Part B-1*, eds. D. L. Wise, D. J. Trantolo, D. E. Altobelli, J. D., Yaszemiski Gresser and E. R. Schwartz (New York: Marcel Dekker), 3–42, 1995.

Yao S. S., Jin F. L., Rhee K. Y., Hui D. and Park, S. J. Recent advances in carbon-fiber-reinforced thermoplastic composites: A review. *Composites Part B: Engineering*, 142, 241–250, 2018.

Zhuang X., Gehrig D., Forler N., Liang H., Wagner M., Hansen M. R., Laquai F., Zhang F. and Feng X. Conjugated microporous polymers with dimensionality-controlled heterostructures for green energy devices. *Advanced Materials,* 27, 3789–3796, 2015.

Index

A

Acetylation treatment, 25
Advantages of natural fiber composites, 7
Alkaline treatment, 25
Applications of natural fibers, 35
Applications of sustainable composites, 82

B

Bamboo, 6
Benzoylation treatment, 26
Biodegradability, 38

C

Characterization of natural fiber, 11–18
Chemical composition of fibers, 35
Chemical treatment, 25
Coconut fiber, 6
Comparison of tribological properties, 75
Composites 11
Compo casting, 67
Compressive strength, 19
Cotton, 7
Crashworthiness, 19

D

Date palm, 6
Disadvantages of natural fiber composites, 11
Double stir casting, 67

E

Economic perspective, 37
Effect of fiber orientation, 33, 68
Effect of fiber loading, 35
Effect of nano material, 52
Effect of operating conditions, 72
Environmental perspective, 36
Extraction of natural fibers 11

F

Fabrication techniques, 11, 62
Fiber concentration, 45
Fiber dispersion, 51
Fiber orientation, 48
Fiber treatment, 51
Flax, 5
Flexural test, 19

Functionalization of polymers and natural fibers, 31

H

Hardness test, 19
Hemp, 3

I

Impact test, 19
Interfacial adhesion between fiber and matrix, 33

J

Jute, 3

K

Kapok, 6
Kenaf, 3

L

Life-cycle assessment, 52

M

Manufacturing process, 35
Mechanical performance, 18
Morphological observation, 16

N

Nettle, 5

P

Peroxide treatment, 26
Physical treatment, 24
Physical properties, 16
Pineapple leaf, 5
Potassium permanganate ($KMnO_4$) treatment, 26
Powder metallurgy, 62
Properties of natural fibers, 7

R

Ramie, 5

S

Silk, 7
Silane treatment, 25

93

Sisal, 6
Sliding speed, 35
Sliding distance, 35
Sliding direction, 35
Stearic acid treatment, 26
Stir casting, 67
Sustainability of NFRC, 35
Sustainable composites for energy applications, 85
Sustainable composites in automobile industry, 82
Sustainable composites in civil structures, 82
Sustainable composites in medical industry, 83
Sustainable composites for miscellaneous
  applications, 88

Sustainable metallic composites, 62
Sustainable polymer composites, 68

T

Tensile test, 18
Thermal behavior, 17
Tribological performance, 20, 67
Type of fiber, 33
Type of polymer, 33

W

Wear mechanisms, 67, 73